The BeCollaboration Story:
Making of a Movement

FEAR   SCARCITY   COMPETITION

to

LOVE   CONNECTION   ABUNDANCE

Gill Tiney

To Terry

Wishing you every success as you begin your BeCollaboration journey

love + best wishes

Gill x

First publishedby BE A Voice in 2017.

Design, typesetting and printing by:
Catalyst Image Solutions: Tel: 020 8524 0791

Printed on acid-free paper from managed forests.
This book is printed on demand, so no copies will be remaindered or pulped.

ISBN No: 978-0-9574201-2-0

Contents

Foreword

by Chief Sharer, Benita Matofska

To share is to be human.

For the last decade, I've been fascinated by the idea of building a society and economic system based around the sharing of human and physical resources – a Sharing Economy[1]. It makes no sense to me that whilst we have more than £3.5 trillion worth of idle resources worldwide[2] – food, homes and clothing; 40,000 people die each day because they can't access these very same necessities[3]. A Sharing Economy, not only makes efficient use of resources by matching surplus with need, but also enables a culture where collaboration, cooperation and co-creation are the norm.

The fact that population growth is leading to a global crisis and the end of planet earth as we know it, is well documented; but I believe, there's a solution that every single one of us can be part of. Though our resources may be finite, each one of us has unlimited capacity to share and collaborate and if we can unleash our collective sharing potential, there's no end to what we can achieve. Far from being some kind of utopian, idealistic dream, this idea is becoming a reality and is causing the biggest societal shift since the Industrial Revolution and the biggest business trend of all time.

Since 2008, which saw the birth of what is now commonly known as the 'Sharing Economy', we've seen the proliferation of sharing initiatives enabling us to access and share everything from homes to humour. Our very notions of ownership, hierarchies, power, work and indeed life, have been turned upside down. In this 'Age of Sharing', our desire and ability to collaborate has never been more significant.

By building a network of collaborators who know that a different world based on the principles of sharing, putting people and planet at the heart of a system that is rooted in fairness, trust and love, BeCollaboration becomes an important part of the solution. This book demonstrates that when we collaborate, anything (yes anything) is possible.

---

[1] Sharing Economy definition by Benita Matofska, 2011
http://www.thepeoplewhoshare.com/blog/what-is-the-sharing-economy/

[2] The People Who Share, 2015

[3] Share the World's Resources, 2014

Benita Matofska, Chief Sharer, 2017

Benita Matofska is a keynote speaker, global Sharing Economy expert and Founder of social enterprise The People Who Share. The People Who Share helps people and companies participate in the Sharing Economy.

Thank you Benita,

To Share AND to collaborate is Humanity at its' Best!

Dedication

To the BeCollaboration community,

you keep my dreams for a better world alive,

with you everything is possible.

Prologue

by Erkan Ali, Creator and Co-Founder of BeCollaboration

"What do you want to be when you grow up…?"

A mindless question we have all been asked as children, my response, "whatever I want!"

"Don't you want to be a doctor or lawyer…?"

"No….what listen to people going on about their problems and illnesses, no thanks!"

And there in lies the rub, what I heard, in that statement, was sacrifice your life for money, status, security and stability, but most importantly get the respect and admiration of others. For many years I would be asked when are you going to get a proper job, and my response would always be "never….I don't want a job!"

Perhaps you can start to see why school was just not for me, and I never saw my life's purpose being expressed within that limited format, never!

So, fast forward to BeCollaboration!

I have always considered myself a maverick, a person of TRUE Integrity, such lines as 'to thine own self be true' to 'can you disappoint another to be true to yourself?' resonated with me.

Well…can you?

Can you 'follow your bliss' as Joseph Campbell stated? Well, I have, I did and I do… the opportunity to make my life about the benefit and forwarding of the human species is what I chose.

For most, it will sound too grand, too unrealistic, even delusional. Inherent for most is the cynicism and resignation that tells them nothing will ever change, or can change, it's just too big and who am I to make that difference? So, for most, they choose career, money, status, stuff, experiences or the other way, they sell out, get depressed and end up in all sorts of difficulties. I believe the system just wants you in debt and paying taxes, like a good little slave.

Taking the 'red pill'[4] has unleashed more in me than I can convey in these words. I have seen behind the curtain. I have worked out many of life's riddles. I have

---

[4] Reference to The Matrix film

unwound the Gordian Knot. Yes there is always more to find out, there are always new discoveries ahead.

And for now….there is BeCollaboration. The opportunity to make an impact, right here and right now, to take my life and the lives of others, who choose to explore, to their next level. To create and build a community predicated on Collaboration for one reason and one reason only, the survival of the species. In this community, we are evolving an emerging consciousness, a break from Fear, Scarcity and Competition to a new empowering context of Love, Connection and Abundance.

So, to answer the question, what do you want to BE when you grow up?

My answer, a **Human Being 1st** everything else comes after.

BeCollaboration is a community where you will uncover a personal journey of discovery and possibility and in this book, Gill Tiney my 'Grand Accomplice' shares her unique and insightful perspective of our journey so far. I am sure you will be challenged and intrigued by her approach, and most importantly, inspired to take another look at your life, your passions and your dreams.

Preface

*Never doubt that a small group of thoughtful, committed citizens
can change the world; indeed, it's the only thing that ever has.*

Margaret Mead

Here is the problem. Do you ever feel that there should be more to life, that something is missing and that for far too many people on our planet life is just plain unfair?

How do you feel when you see the latest news? You know it isn't right that children are starving in the world, and wars are run by people who are nowhere near the countries they are devastating. You know that even in your own country, cruel people enslave women for sex and groom children for the sick and perverted pleasures of others.

How do you feel when you consider that narcotic drugs are illegal and yet our food chain is supplemented by chemicals that are killing us? Does it make you despair that even today women are paid less than men for doing the same job? How do you feel knowing that our health service and public transport are breaking under the strain of underfunding? And let's not even mention the toxic effects of Brexit and Donald Trump!

In this digital age it is no longer possible to pretend these things are not happening. Every day we are bombarded by problems in our world. Is it any wonder mental illness is on the rise and some days we can't even get out of bed? Yet what can we do? How can we as individuals make a difference? Surely, one person cannot even make a dent in all this awfulness.

Then there are those rare days when you just know that you can no longer sit on the side lines. You get this overwhelming feeling that it is no longer okay to simply send a text to donate some money to a worthy cause. You cannot ignore the call any longer, sometimes you need to be part of that cause. One injustice too many, one personal fight with authority, or clash with cancer finds you searching; searching to make a difference with your life, searching to leave a legacy, a need to make your mark on this planet and leave it in a better state than you found it.

That urgency, the full realisation that time is running out, and that we simply HAVE to make a difference to this complacent, indifferent, damaged world – that was the moment when BeCollaboration was born.

One person had that realisation, knowing that he could no longer sit on the side lines. What he saw, and what others had been telling us for a long time, is that our world was being run for the benefit of the few, at huge cost to the many. NOW was the time to take some action. He just knew that on his own he could not accomplish very much. He needed to surround himself with people who were on the same mission. He knew in his heart that when he was joined with others, sharing his passion he would be stronger, be able to make an impact, and know that his vision could be realised.

He began the search for his first follower. Someone who would be as angry as he was at the way the world was being run. Someone who felt a sense of urgency that something had to change. Someone who believed that intrinsically everyone was fundamentally good, but we had allowed complacency, greed, ignorance and fear to permeate and get a foothold. Someone who was ready to roll up their sleeves and get stuck in to create a movement focused on collaboration, where people were seen simply as a Human Being. He didn't care if they were British or Turkish, black or white, male or female, gay or straight, rich or poor, able or disabled, clever or stupid. All they had to be was simply a wonderful, beautiful, genius of a Human Being and ready to make an impact on the world around them.

I signed up.[5]

As a mother of two, married for 30+ years and small time entrepreneur, I was at that time in my life where I was ready to acknowledge that I could no longer ignore what I was seeing all around me. I didn't want to admit that I was guilty of allowing my world to deteriorate around me. I had to do something – at this stage I didn't know what, but doing nothing just didn't feel comfortable anymore.

I committed myself to live in action to make this a better planet. I saw collaboration as the way forward, the missing link that would transform the way the world works together. Because of my background in business networking, I knew I had the skills to bring together passionate people to work to make the world a better place. I had no idea where this idea might lead, or what I would be expected to do, or where it would take me. All I knew was that doing nothing was no longer an option.

---

[5] Ironically 'signing up' was a symbolic handshake. Initially Collaborators joined us with the same ethos, we didn't feel the need to conform to legal documents in order to work together to support each other. At the time of writing I am proud to say no one has felt the need to ask for a written agreement. The trust that is built superseded the need for protecting oneself with legal documents. To date no Collaborator has signed an agreement, no legal relationship exists, just the simple verbal agreement to work collaboratively to share, support, encourage and further the knowledge of what it means to work in a collaborative environment for the good of humanity.

The person who had these crazy ideas that inspired me so much, was born in the UK, of Turkish Cypriot parents. In his younger day Erkan Ali used to consider all white people racist, and in his culture women were not viewed as equal. He spent years working on his own personal development, learning to see the world as much as possible without filters or bias, and looking back now, the irony does not escape him when he acknowledges that in pursuing the biggest mission of his life, he is partnered with a white English woman!

Human Being First

> "It takes a village to raise a child, it takes a BeCollaboration community to transform an adult."
>
> **[Erkan Ali 2015]**

In our world of supposed great sophistication and enlightenment, being born black or gay or disabled shouldn't make any difference to a child, or determine whether they have a good education, prospects or the opportunity to have a good and meaningful life. Sadly, we know that this is not the case.

That is why within BeCollaboration our core values identify what is important to us. It is not about what a person brings with them as a Collaborator - it is *what they can become*. We look on all of our Collaborators as a Human Being First. That is to say, we don't care if they are an accountant, a web designer, or someone who is unemployed. All of us have dreams and desires to help someone, and therefore all are welcome.

There is an example I want to share, because to me it is the epitome of the type of person we attract. One of our Collaborators asked if he could bring a friend to a meeting. Naturally we said yes. He then explained that he had only met this friend on New Year's Eve and that this person was homeless. Joe duly turned up at our regular monthly meeting and was met with open arms (quite literally). He had been given some new clothes and had made a huge effort to be part of the group. He was quite visibly nervous, and admitted he very nearly didn't come as he thought he would have nothing in common with anyone. He was genuinely scared of what to expect, yet after the meeting he stayed to chat some more and was blown away by the friendliness and interest in his position. Throughout the meeting I saw him visibly grow and relax when he realised this was a safe space to be around genuine people. By the time he left two of our Collaborators had offered him a job. With the help of Facebook, his situation was soon spread further and he was offered accommodation too.

All because one of our Collaborators was kind enough to invite him along.

I am passionate about equality, I strongly believe that we all have a duty to help everyone if they are prepared and ready to help themselves. The Para Olympics have given all of us a great example to follow. If you can start working towards your dreams within a BeCollaboration community, then you have others who are ready to help you. There can be no excuse for not giving it a go.

Most people down on their luck just need someone to believe in them, to be prepared to help them and remind them that they are important. We can all do that for someone can't we? When I talk about BeCollaboration I explain that it is a community who are out to make a difference, maybe on a world-wide scale but more often simply to the person sitting next to them. It doesn't have to be a massive difference, but quite often by taking small regular steps towards making a small difference, you can look back and see a major impact has occurred without you ever realising it. We want to make the world a better place and if that means by helping one person at a time, then so be it. One person alone will make a small dent, but a whole community across the world will create harmony and peace.

In the words of Martin Luther King *"I have a dream"* that one day when BeCollaboration is a global organisation known for creating possibility out of seeming impossible odds, I get summoned to meet with Donald Trump, and sit him down and explain that instead of building a wall with Mexico, he needs to build bridges with the rest of the world. I see life in very simplistic terms. There is no problem on this planet that I believe cannot be solved, we just have to be open to possibility.

Yet one person on their own simply isn't enough. I see a BeCollaboration group in every town, in every school, in every country, meeting regularly. Placing everyone as a Human Being First, following a culture based on collaboration, connection and transformation of the species creating love and acceptance wherever they go - surely that is what we all want isn't it?

We are citizens in a globalized world, working towards peace, unity and love. We have a vision to teach and share our knowledge for the benefit of all. We have a vision of creating a way of BEing for future generations; a place where harmony exists, communication is positive and proactive and we all work towards solving problems on the basis of a win/win/win solution.

Seems obvious, doesn't it?

1.
A Grown-Up Conversation

As a society, as human beings we are highly conditioned. It is with this reality that I begin this chapter on the context for the BeCollaboration conversation.

"The Shift Age"

Back in 1996 we were told by *Graciela Chichilnisky in a paper in the Journal of International Trade and Economic Development* that we are experiencing the "Knowledge Revolution":[6]

> *'Knowledge is an intangible public good. It is privately produced, and it is replacing land and machines as the primary factors of production prevailing in the agricultural and industrial revolutions. This alters the terms of the debate between capitalism and socialism, and leads to a human-centred society with different types of markets, corporate structure and financial structures'.*

In the last five years we have also been told by many business 'experts' that we are experiencing an "Entrepreneur Revolution": there have never been as many entrepreneurs as at this moment in history.

It doesn't take long to dig below the surface to find that many people see that we are living in amazing times. David Houle the evolutionary geneticist, believes we are in what he describes as "The Shift Age". He looks back to a time when change was a generational activity, when new technology such as the dishwasher would take 10 – 20 years to even cross the ocean from US to UK households. Now we appear to be in a constant state of change. You only have to look at the technology around you to know that it constantly needs updating. Even if you don't want to update your mobile phone, eventually you find that it becomes obsolete – you have no choice but to buy a new one. Most people my age, in the baby boomer generation, do not relish change and look back fondly to a time when life seemed slower, easier.

Incredible changes are occurring in all areas of life, from driverless cars, currently not a common sight on our roads, to 3D printers that are becoming more common place. Science fiction evolves into science fact, with news that Artificial Intelligence in Japan has been used to create a life size version of US actress Scarlett Johannson to be a hotel receptionist! What will they think of next? However, the permutations do not bode well when we hear stories of care homes being a primary market for

---

[6] Columbia University Discussion **Paper** series.

these type of robots. Can you imagine your incapacitated parents being cared for by a robot? Loneliness is the epidemic that we are creating, the disease that will spread as technology indiscriminately isolates us.

Lynda Gratton who wrote *The Shift: The Future of Work is Already Here* describes how life might look in 2025 if technology continues at the current pace. Her picture is not encouraging, yet how can we welcome such advances while still balancing the need to be human?

We are in a time in history like no other. Where technology teaches technology, robots become everyday companions, whole industries become obsolete and 'Big Brother' is watching our every move. Have you even begun to consider how that will affect you and your family?

We have already seen supermarkets begin to replace cashiers with automated kiosks, and self check-in at airports. We have seen Uber taxis summoned by an app, and the world's largest provider of holiday accommodation - Airbnb - taking on the giants of the hotel industry without owning a single hotel. All these innovations threaten unemployment for millions of people with a predicted unemployment rate of 48%.

For many, technology is robbing us of jobs. Could that be a good thing with consideration by some countries of a Universal Basic Income as described by Peter Diamandis on his blog **https://www.linkedin.com/pulse/universal-basic-income-peter-diamandis**

The Education System

Education is stuck in a system that was developed for the Industrial Revolution of the late 18th century. The Victorians developed it further to support the great manufacturing boom. Our children today are still learning within a system that is by and large not fit for purpose. Remembering facts and figures is not as important as it once was, because we now have a new verb, to 'Google'. The unevolved education system does not predominantly test understanding, it is simply looking to grade memory.

What education needs to adapt to is the 'why' and the 'how'. How does something happen and more importantly – WHY.

If children can become problem-solvers and versed in how to communicate effectively, they will be able to function well in today's society. The most pre-eminent transitional skill for everyone, is to be able to communicate effectively, and yet this doesn't appear to be measured within the current tests, because the system does not consider it of value.

One hundred years ago, we kind of knew where we stood. If you were born into a poor family you only had a couple of options to escape. If you were born into a professional family where your father was a doctor or a lawyer, the chances were - if you were a boy - you would follow your dad into the family profession. If you were a girl that choice did not exist, but you were expected to marry well.

Now the world is a very different place. We do have choices. We have options and to a large extent, there is in theory at least, that education is for all and that we have some degree of choice as to what profession we claim for our future.

If only it were that simple. If education held the key to our future happiness we would all study hard at school, get good jobs and have a fulfilling life – wouldn't we? Well let's just test that theory a little more.

- Not all children have access to an equally good level of education

- We do not all start from an even playing field

- Where we are born has a significant impact on our opportunities (and I'm only thinking about the UK at this stage)

- Where we grow up also has a significant impact on us, from the quality of schools to the funding of our local NHS

- Whether we are able bodied, matters;

- Whether we have a mental illness or disability

- Whether we are boy or girl

- What our sexual orientation is

- What the colour of our skin is

- Whether our parents claim benefits

- Whether our parents have been to prison

- Whether we have parents at all

- Whether we have spent some time in care

- Whether our parents/carers are in debt

And this is just the tip of the iceberg.

What could our education system look like? What should it look like? Have we even invented one school that comes close? Ricardo Semlar has made a start see his Ted Talk **http://lumiar.org.br/index.php/a-escola/?lang=en**

Scarcity v. Abundance

We acknowledge the prevailing thinking, that in particular dominates the Western World, that constantly reinforces a fear of scarcity rather than acknowledging abundance. Apparently, we are running out – of everything! Have you seen the news lately? Not enough oil, not enough money, not enough food, not enough water. And yet some countries have them in abundance, so much so that they have food going to waste, water that can supply islands from the sea and billionaires aplenty.

What we really have is a distribution problem. There are way too many people not receiving anywhere near a fair share. Oxfam [7] recently released figures that illustrated that 64 of the world's richest people have more money than 3.64 billion of the world's population. That is over half of the world's population!

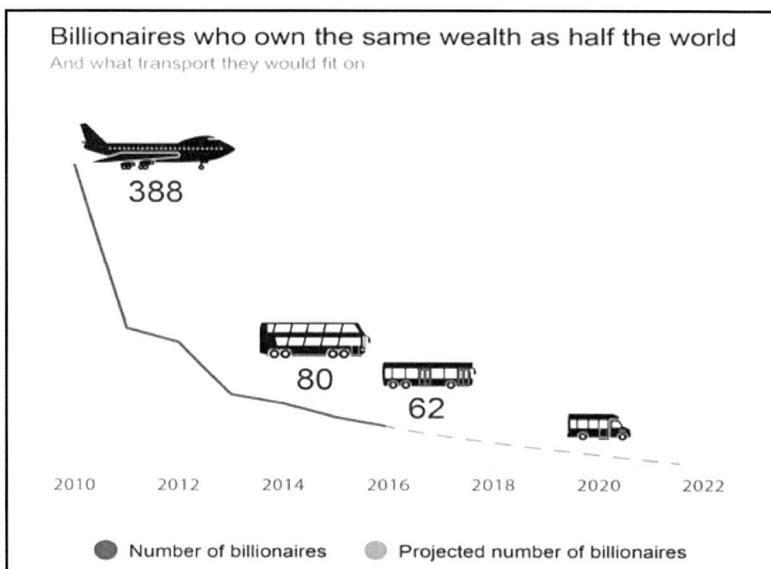

Billionaires who own the same wealth as half the world
And what transport they would fit on

388

80

62

2010   2012   2014   2016   2018   2020   2022

● Number of billionaires   ● Projected number of billionaires

---

[7] http://www.oxfam.org.uk/media-centre/press-releases/2016/01/62-people-own-same-as-half-world-says-oxfam-inequality-report-davos-world-economic-forum

Am I the only one who feels shocked to the core at what those figures represent? The problem is not shortage; the problem is distribution. Whilst conspiracy theories abound, I am not here to expose those who are doing wrong, (that is a whole other book about tax dodging corporations and gun running governments). I am simply here to highlight the fact that we do not have to accept that this is the way it is supposed to be. Together we have a voice and together we can make a difference. Even money-making corporate machines have the ability to leave a legacy that has a lasting positive impact to the lives of billions of people. Don't we all want that?

Ultimately, we want our Collaborators to make a stand that says we are not okay with the status quo. In other words, it is not right that;

- Our children come out of university education with massive debts
- That men often still earn more than women for doing the same job
- That pharmaceutical companies are selling us drugs when cures can be had from simply altering your diet
- That genetically modified foods are entering our food stream without our knowledge
- That our water system is overloaded with hormones
- That there is more slavery in the world today than at any time in the 18th and 19th centuries

and much more.

Have you worked it out yet? BeCollaboration is not some cosy club of concerned people working out how to put on a coffee morning for a charity. We seriously want to work out how we can make an impact on the planet: an impact to stop some of the inequalities, violence and corruption we hear about on a daily basis.

What do we leave behind?

We all get to a certain time in our lives when we feel we should be giving back. Making our time on this planet worthwhile; leaving it in a better state than we found it, for our children and future generations. This is why, I feel, BeCollaboration resonates with so many. They do not feel able to make an impact alone, so they have a greater chance if they team-up with other like-minded souls. Collaborators join us not always knowing what they can offer, or not even sure if their idea is too mad or simply not possible. All they know is that there is an overriding intuition that compels them to seek a way forward.

We believe that together we are stronger and together a solution can occur that individually would not and could not have been discovered. We know from scientific research and books such as *The Click* by Ori and Rom Brafman, that by understanding how people click, and bringing people together, human beings generate unique opportunities and influence to make things happen. This is embedded in the way we are made and was brilliantly illustrated by Professor Jill Bolte-Taylor, when she explained that by bringing both our left (analytical) and right (creative) brains to problem solving, we produce phenomenal results. [8]

Bringing people together follows the same principle. We have people passionate about education, conservation, entrepreneurialism, mindfulness, healing, consciousness, finance and fitness, among others. All have found others to connect with and make a start on their contribution. It does not have to be a massive project and it does not have to have an end in sight. As long as they are moving towards making that difference, others will come along – some way in the future to support them so their ideas can also be nurtured and grown along the way. We don't have to have all the answers, but we do need to keep asking the questions, so work towards solving the unsolvable. That is how it works.

Fear and Love

In developing BeCollaboration we have always looked back into the course of history to ask why has this idea not taken hold before. We looked at theories that spread over time and geography, populations and individuals. Books such as Robert Wright's *Non Zero: The Logic of Human Destiny,* and Michael R. Drew and Roy H. Williams *Pendulum - How Past Generations Shape Our Present and Predict Our Future,* were both significant in understanding how this current paradigm evolved and how we might shape the future to create something better.

One theory that resonated with us was Spiral Dynamics, originally formulated by Clare Graves but continued after his death by Don Beck.[9] This fascinating theory

---

[8] http://www.ted.com/talks/jill_bolte_taylor_s_powerful_stroke_of_insight In the powerful Ted Talk by Jill Bolte Taylor, we learn how powerful our brains are and how beautiful our world becomes when we harness both sides of our brain.

[9] I urge you to look further into this fascinating subject. See https://www.architectural-review.com/rethink/campaigns/the-big-rethink/the-big-rethink-part-10-spiral-dynamics-and-culture/8638840.article *"The last several decades have seen the emergence, across a number of fields, of modes of developmental thinking whereby species and eco-systems, people and cultures, and even consciousness are seen to evolve through identifiable developmental stages."*[9][Peter Buchanan, 2012]

describes, among other things, why religion hasn't quite been able to unite our communities. As we searched for why the vision of BeCollaboration – something so obvious – had not worked we began to see that the picture was much more complex.

We could see that churches, synagogues, mosques, and places of worship do to some extent fulfil the need we see: they are centres of community, playing a role in helping and supporting. But as a force for uniting community they appear on some levels to divide. With a focus on religious practice, rules and doctrines they can feel like an exclusive club rather than an inclusive community. Importantly many are structured around a fear based ideology, that if you go against a doctrine then punishment will follow. Over the decades religion has a lot to answer for: that is why I believe the answer to the world's problems is not religion. [10]

As humankind has evolved over time we have grouped ourselves according to our needs. Going back to the Maslows' hierarchy of needs, stone-age Man was focused on survival. In Spiral Dynamics, survival is described as instinctive, and survivalist. As time has moved on we have moved up the spiral, and appear in the 21st Century to be around the orange/green level, between strategic and egalitarian in purpose. When looked at from a geographical perspective, we in the Western World are higher up the spiral, and moving towards yellow (in some areas) whilst in parts of the Middle-East there is a strong blue level, focused on authoritarian religious doctrine.

When taken at the level of the individual, it is possible to identify people you may know who are happiest when they are on a spending spree (orange), while other friends are content and happiest when working for their charity, perhaps on a conservation project. Here they would be identified as egalitarian, (green).

---

[10] It is my personal belief – and I am not speaking on behalf of any other Collaborator - that faith is a wonderful, empowering concept and whatever way people choose to support their faith is fine as long as they do not try to indoctrinate anyone else. No one can give you faith, you have to choose it for yourself. Faith is spiritual and religion is man-made. You have to go where you feel it is *right* for you not because you are scared *not* to go.

Turquoise:
Holistic Meme

Yellow:
Integrative Meme

Green:
Communitarian
Egalitarian

Orange:
Achievist
Strategic

Blue:
Purposeful
Authoritarian

Red:
Impulsive
Egocentric

Purple:
Magical
Animistic

Beige:
Instinctive
Survivalistic

Once you can have identified where you are on the spectrum, you can see more clearly how you are a product of your surroundings. With awareness comes clarity and the system helps with highlighting the drivers that currently guide your life. When you broaden it out into looking at your society as a whole, the picture becomes very interesting. Have you worked it out yet? It is amazing once you see it: the vast majority of the population are driven by FEAR!

What we see everywhere is FEAR! A fear of not getting my share, of not living up to expectations, of having to strive daily to earn a crust. Fear of not being able to pay the mortgage, of watching our backs, doing enough to get by, of not getting 'what I deserve' my 'rights', fear of not being respected, not being understood. Fear of not being good enough.

Sound familiar?

Coming from this place of scarcity, is it any wonder collaboration doesn't happen? It's stifled before it can even get a foothold. We are indoctrinated to not trust anyone, look after number one, as apparently nobody else will, because (as we are told) 'it's a dog eat dog world'. Why would we collaborate? If we work solo we have no one else to consider or worry about.

The fear conversation is constantly ringing loud and clear in practically every conversation, every thought.

Fear   Love

And yet....

We are finding small groups of people who are ready, like never before, to help each other, support each other, without any personal agenda, simply from the goodness of their hearts. This is already out there: people want to live like this, and are ready to transform, to fulfil their fundamental need deep within them – to make a difference. To live from a place where financial reward is of no consequence and doing the *right* thing from a spiritual and moral view is favoured.

In other words, to live from a place of LOVE rather than fear. To embrace the human race as one, and to bring good ideas together for the benefit of each other and the wider community.

This is my world, where I know lovely people who do amazing acts of kindness for others, without any need for payback. People who believe in Karma, the universal bank account, or more simply, being kind because it makes them feel good. Did you ever try smiling to a stranger, making small talk, brightening someone's day? It pays back tenfold. I do this not because I am an extrovert or have a need for validation, or want to be noticed. I do it simply because it makes me feel happy to bring a smile to someone's face and tell them something good about themselves.

Here is another story:

I was in the supermarket check-out the other day and got talking to an elderly gentleman who was moaning that his wife should be doing this for him. I smiled and told him it was his good deed for the day. He then opened up and said he was a carer for his wife and he loved taking care of her but shopping was his least favourite task. In that case you are building up lots of brownie points, I told him and I hope that my husband is as kind to me as you are to your very lucky wife. He beamed and chuckled 'you wouldn't say that if you tasted my cooking'. We both left smiling with a different view on our own worlds, and the cashier was grinning too.

I felt he wasn't used to people engaging in conversation with him. His world is very difficult and he probably feels incredibly lonely tackling tasks that were traditionally ones he never expected to learn. He is isolated, as no doubt are many others and possibly desperately lonely. It is the epidemic of our modern world. I see collaboration and in particular BeCollaboration as a solution to this tragic consequence of the constant shifts of our time.

Speed of change

At no time since the Industrial Revolution have we experienced such rapid change. Indeed, Daniel Priestley CEO of DENT explains in his book *Entrepreneur Revolution* how he sees this amazing period transforming the landscape of business.

> *"The slow dinosaurs of the industrial age are being outpaced by fast-moving start-ups, ambitious small businesses and technological innovators."*

He speaks of the massive opportunities that are available to the entrepreneur because of the innovations that are coming to us. Simply looking at the innovation all around us we cannot help but be daunted by the possible repercussions. What will the impact of the latest technologies be? To learn that it is now possible to use 3D printing to manufacture houses made from recycled materials is extraordinary. It is no longer impossible to imagine that the same technology could be used to print blood and organs. Robotics in the form of biotech is moving forward in leaps and bounds and augmented reality may dispense with the need for a mobile phone (Hurrah!). Will we bemoan the loss of our device or revel in our high tech specs?

As I write Peter Diamondis Executive Chairman of the X Prize Foundation has announced the launch of the first true quantum computers, which will give us vast computing power based on the memory of atoms and molecules. "The implications of true quantum computing" he says are staggering, and will have an "extraordinary impact to society today".

A lot of the jobs and even industries we currently know will become extinct. A taxi ride will potentially be taken over by a driverless car. An accountant will have 90% of his normal tasks and calculations completed by artificial intelligence. These innovations will disrupt industries and reduce the employability of our current workforce. Many of us will face unemployment, or under-employment. Many more could become unemployable, unless we can adapt. Is this a welcome change? Are you an accountant cheering about the fact you will no longer have to do the tax returns, or do you feel shocked that your role could be defunct?

Generally, we find that people are split into two camps. In one camp are those who are shocked by the devastation of the job market and who visualise riots in the street, akin to the Miners strikes in the 1970's. And in the other are those who see a whole new world where we embrace employment in areas we do not yet even know exist.

We live in an age where connectivity to the internet makes it possible for us to have a global company and yet have no office. We can have hundreds of people working for us, yet have no employees. As the old paradigm of what it means to 'go to work' is totally changing, we see that people, our most precious resource, are being side-lined in the race to the next technology. We believe that BeCollaboration has emerged at the right time for two reasons:

FIRST: If machines run the mundane parts of our lives, we now have a duty to explore the BE-ing of every person. Who are they Being, what do they want to achieve, what is their destiny? By teaching every person to understand their Being, who they are and what their purpose is, we empower everyone to contribute their best to society in this ever-changing and to some, a scary new world.

SECOND: Collaboration is about working together to build a better world, supporting each other, looking for the genius in everyone and building a community for the benefit of all. By redefining what collaboration is, sharing how to collaborate effectively, creating a whole new paradigm for what it means to do business together, we create a flexible, fluid, structure that can withstand and move within our shifting and constantly changing world. With our culture and core values at our centre, we will establish the structure to provide growth on a personal, commercial and environmental level. As one member of the community described it 'BeCollaboration simply enables me to be the best me I can be'.

We want to amplify those words, and those feelings into all areas of the globe, and the time is NOW!

Why now?

Surely the best time to bring unity and equality would have been immediately after the Second World War. We are told by our parents who experienced some of the atrocities, that it was indeed a time of unity and unparalleled community but seeing how societies evolved we know it didn't last. The frugal fifties gave way to the swinging sixties and before we realised it the yuppie eighties were among us and life became an insular *'what's in it for me'* (WIIFM) society.

We have all been swept along by the media telling us how to think and behave. The belief that attainment of stuff buys happiness and travel to far flung places is essential in order to tick off an ever increasing bucket list. To what end? What makes this the right time to bring society back to a place of community, to a space of inner peace, of happiness through spiritual fulfilment and empathy towards species?

Whether you believe in the law of attraction, a higher being or simply synchronicity, at BeCollaboration we have found that evidence keeps appearing before us to show us that this is THE time to collaborate and build a strong community for the benefit of all.

The key to understanding why now, is understanding the speed of change. Earlier in this chapter I mentioned the futurist David Houle, author of *The Shift Age.* [11] In it Houle explains that never in our history have we experienced such a phenomenal rate of change. It is now constant and we have to prepare ourselves for the fundamental ongoing shift in every aspect of our lives. In the past, change has happened and we adjusted our lives to fit. Today it is constant and we need to be perpetually moving forward in order to keep up.

I also mentioned Lynda Gratton, the organizational theorist and Professor at London Business School. In her book Gratton[12] writes of a constantly changing world, where super-connectivity will enable diversity, skill sharing and a world without boundaries. She describes what the world of employment might look like in 2025 across the world and highlights the hidden dangers of isolation and loneliness. She acknowledges that this is the biggest shift in our working life since the Industrial Revolution, highlighting the fact that 5 generations will be part of the workforce with people living to 100+. This will fundamentally drive change in how we function as humans, as societies operate. She believes that with innovation changing our work practices, how we connect and work together will constantly develop, and with it will come the need to adapt to the everchanging shifts in the way we do things.

---

[11] For a synopsis of his thinking see David Houle - www.youtube.com/watch?v=3K5hojsS-48

[12] A useful synopsis of her book can be found by the author at
www.youtube.com/watch?v=XuAzulObY9s

If the 'doing' is going to be in constant change then our 'Being' needs be grounded to support our communities in this everchanging world.[13]

Charles Leadbeater a leading authority on innovation and creativity and author of *We Think,* also highlighted how dynamic 'group think' has been newly enabled by the internet, but is not limited to online activity. He illustrates via an experiment on the internet called 'I Love Bees', a mystery that engaged thousands in group think online, but which also manifested in physical space.[14] Thousands of people solved the mystery and no one did so for cash. They engaged because it was fun and were motivated by how such mobilisation could be used for good. If such an energy of group think were enabled within a community with strong core values and was powered by love so much could be possible.

The more I research the more I am comforted to find I am not alone in my realisation that the time is NOW.

We have to create a new way of BEing in order to operate within a new paradigm and support those who will be affected. Community is often missing and Collaboration will bring us back together again.

It only takes a few people to start the ball rolling.

In fact in the beginning it is the only thing that ever has...

---

[13] Also see *Pendulum* by Michael R. Drew and Roy H. Williams mentioned in the last chapter also offers us an insight into how society changes every 80 years and swings from a 'me' society to a 'we' society. They argue that memes are created whereby we assimilate into a society's consciousness a world where we are all for one, or out for only me.

[14] See 'I Love Bees' https://www.youtube.com/watch?v=SNhurUnOWKQ

2.

The Lone Nut

On the 21st March 2012 my Life changed. I was attending a Neuro Linguistic Programming (NLP) course run by David Key. During the lunchbreak I decided to find out more about my fellow attendees, and one person in particular seemed very opinionated and intense in his observations. I noticed the others move slowly away from our conversation as the subject level deepened from 'what did you think of the morning?' to 'where do you think money comes from' and don't you realise that there is a conspiracy to keep us all as slaves?'

His style was similar to many old school sales consultants who aim to make you feel stupid so that you eventually feel you should buy their services. I secretly wondered how I too could get away. I assumed that once he bothered to find out that I too was a business coach he, like many of the other coaches would consider me competition and move away.

As much as I smiled inwardly at his views on the monetary system, I was intrigued at his passion for the bigger subjects: there was no space for small talk in his repertoire. He did eventually ask about what I did for a living and surprisingly became engaged in the conversation even more, this time asking me lots of questions "What did I love most about it? What did I consider to be my sweet spot? Did I collaborate with anyone? What were my ambitions? Did I always work alone?"

At the end of lunch he suggested meeting up for coffee. To be honest, I was intrigued enough to say yes, but nervous as to what the outcome might be, there was no second guessing this guy.

It was definitely not love at first sight, but whether you believe in serendipity, synchronicity, fate, or the law of attraction, there was something there that compelled me to know more. I had been beavering away to be the best coach I could be, and constantly trying to upgrade my skills, but I always felt overwhelmed at being a small cog in a massive world. What impact could I have? I was doing my best, but being a 'solo-preneur' I knew in the back of my mind I could only help a small number of people. At that time I had satisfied myself that it was 'good enough'. Meeting Erkan sparked the thought "What if you could be more?"

It was probably the first time I had acknowledged to myself that I was playing small. I had been coming from the viewpoint of making money. I never wanted to be decadent, I didn't need much money, and therefore helping people on a one-by-one basis seemed ok.

I was 'good enough', definitely playing safe.

Now, here was a person challenging me to be more. Not for what I could have out of it, but for the people I could help. It was my duty to work out how I can help as many people as possible. He definitely touched a dormant nerve. I always believed I had been put on this planet to raise awesome kids, and if I say so myself – job done! But what now? Surely there are other reasons for me to be here? I'm not meant to potter around the planet helping the odd person here and there – that simply wasn't the plan. I had been hiding from myself, hiding from the possibility of making this a better planet – yes ME! It was time I stepped up, and I didn't have to do it alone.

The first Collaboration on our journey had begun and a very special friendship had been born.

Erkan Ali was was born on 12th July 1968 in North London to Turkish Cypriot parents who had lived through the Greek/Turkish conflict in 1974. By my standards his was a privileged upbringing. His father was in business and ran several dry-cleaning shops. They holidayed in Turkey for one or two months a year and he considered himself a global citizen. The eldest of three, with one sister and one brother, he was confident of life from a very early age.

To all intents and purpose he lived an idyllic lifestyle. At the age of 12 his family moved to the leafy suburbs in Hertfordshire and he started a new school. Having never experienced racism in London, he was shocked on his very first day to be physically assaulted, for no other reason than the colour of his skin. He waspunched in the face, and called a "Paki". The anger that he felt that day was to fuel, for many years, his intense dislike for white people. In his young mind anyone who was white was now racist. As he explains it now, surrounded by friends from all nationalities, it seems ludicrous that this one incident could have clouded his world for so long. And yet, such episodes happen to us all during our lives and cloud our future, without us even realising it.

The young Erkan was always searching. Looking beyond the horizon for what was just out of reach. He was interested in people, what made them tick, what they were interested in and more importantly why. Working from a young age for his father in the dry-cleaning business, he was soon building his reputation for provoking people to think at a deeper level, playing the protagonist and sometimes creating mischief. He quickly learnt the art of business and helped to grow the family business into a huge operation. When his father retired it was natural for Erkan to take over.

While the business was growing he was investigating the world of personal development. Soon he found a place that resonated with him. Having been brought up in a Turkish community where nationalism was expressed as fervently as a religion, and where religion was revered although not necessarily practiced, he was now ready to see what else was out there.

He found Landmark Education and so began his journey to personal freedom. From Landmark, he discovered that the incident at school where he had experienced violent racism had been clouding his judgement, ruling his life and his past had been impacting his future. Once he had come to terms with the power that incident had held over him, his journey to transformation began. As too did his fascination for the whole transformational concept.

Suffering from dyslexia, Erkan found ways to overcome his disability by listening to audio books and watching videos. He found his thirst for learning was insatiable, and he loved learning on his terms. He was not a product of the education system of his time because he rebelled within it and refused to comply with the regulations. He saw them as restrictive and demeaning and counter-productive to his own education. He wanted to choose what he would learn and as the internet grew, so did his appetite for the unusual, the unpredictable and unconventional. He learnt that his way of studying was fuelled in part from an OCD response: the intense drive to know more about a topic. He allowed his research to be random and chaotic, which took him to dark places in the search for knowledge that was true – as opposed to knowledge that was presented as fact. He became very aware that the world we thought we knew was only the tip of the iceberg. He became fascinated by conspiracy theories and stretched his thinking from subjects as diverse as corporate and political corruption to alien landings and flat earth theory.

Within this learning he was unconsciously building up thousands of hours of investigation on transformation, all whilst pursuing his own personal development within Landmark Education. It was not long before they acknowledged his natural talents and asked him to become more involved with the organization.

The touch paper had been lit. With his natural curiosity in people, his desire to make the world a better place and his experience in business it wasn't long before 'Results Business Coach' was born. He embarked upon what he saw as a dream business, helping others realise their purpose and helping them achieve their aspirations.

And yet there was still something missing for him. Working with clients and being part of the team was a great buzz for Erkan. Yet inevitably the time came when his clients thanked him for his input and were ready to move on alone. Erkan felt rejected and knew there was something not quite right.

He loved being part of a team. He loved the dynamics of creativity that evolved within brainstorming sessions. He felt working with a client for 6 months to a year then moving on to the next company left him feeling there was only a job half done. He wanted to add value on a long term basis, for his clients to feel they had more to give rather than measurements being taken purely on turnover or profit. There was a gap and this gap he identified as a heart space in the world in which the era of consumerism, consumption, and self-gratification left many people feeling hollow. He found himself asking, "Is this all there is?" Time and again he came across business owners who were lamenting the same stories "I have made mountains of cash yet I am still unhappy".

What was missing? What would make sense of the world for these people – most people. What is the key? Eventually he realised that the answer had been staring him in the face all the time:

CONTEXT is KEY

Not unsurprisingly when we talk about context to people we find that most understand it on a superficial level, but those who have grasped the full concept can then lead their lives in a more fulfilling and meaningful way.

Erkan explains why context is so important:

> **CONTEXT** has been at the heart of BeCollaboration since before it was created.
>
> **CONTEXT** is there before you are, it's the view, thinking and being that is there before we have the chance to even articulate what is being thought.
>
> For example, what do these words mean to you?
>
> Muslim, Refugee, Immigrant, Accountant, Politician, Bank Manager, Car Dealer, or how about Donald TRUMP?
>
> What these words evoke, is influenced by an invisible force we are referring to as **CONTEXT**, and **CONTEXT is KEY**.
>
> Now try these words,
>
> Customers, Staff, Sales, Marketing, Cash Flow, Time, Traffic, Busy.
>
> Or how about these, my Body, my Mum or Sister, my ex-wife or my Cancer?
>
> Not so easy, eh?

*In the principle of **'BE DO HAVE'** – (Source Landmark Education) it is our being that shapes what is and is not possible, what we can and can't do, what results we can and cannot achieve. In **'BE DO HAVE'**, we are able to identify the hidden force of **CONTEXT**, once identified and altered, created or managed, new possibilities arise as a natural expression.*

*In our current culture there is a **CONTEXT of Fear, Scarcity and Competition.** How we see Education, Money and Media is predicated on it. We are divided and conquered and kept in debt in perpetuity, that's what the infinite growth paradigm creates, hence 'death and taxes,' being the only certainty.*

*At BeCollaboration, we are shifting **CONTEXT** to one of **Love, Connection and Abundance.** By reinventing ourselves in our known Genius, we are creating such a powerful **CONTEXT**, we are transforming what it means to go to work, share and engage with other human beings, the possibilities are endless. We feel it will lead to solving the unsolvable.*

***By Erkan Ali**

When we first met, Erkan was already working on a higher purpose. The 'what if?' questions were already buzzing around in his head

- What if we weren't tainted by the current education system?
- What if people were made aware of how the current paradigm has been made up?
- What if the genius we have within us was unleashed?
- What if I had a community around me that were aware of their inner genius and wanted the world to be a better place?
- What if I were able to make a world where collaboration was the norm instead of the exception?

He had discussed this with others and in particular with his friend and client Naresh Haldipur, who concurred that indeed the time was right for a new way to do business. No longer seen as being in competition with each other but working together for the good of the client. The proverbial win/win/win – for the coach/collaborator, the client and the planet.

To him it seemed obvious and easy. He just had to get the right people around him.

So, when he met me, he was already on a mission to collect talented individuals to support his theory.

We then spent many meetings exploring whether we were truly aligned. He explained his philosophy of context being key to everything and fundamental as the lynchpin of the new business. He used the mnemonic of **'BE DO HAVE'** to illustrate the contextual conversation and in doing so we realised that not only was *collaboration* pivotal in the process, but our BEing was fundamental in the success of every collaboration. How can we collaborate if our BEing is not authentic and genuine, if we don't aspire to be better human beings and have the interest of others as our default setting?

We both agreed that we do not care what people DO for a living, it does not define them. What matters is who are they Being? What are they making a stand for, what impact do they want to have on the world?

What we wanted to know was what they loved doing; what made them leap out of bed in the morning, what made them furious, what would drive them to action. More importantly we wanted to know what they wanted to leave behind, what impact they wanted to make on our planet, what legacy did they see was theirs? Did they even know yet? Would they like to know, would they like to find out with us?

It soon became very clear that not only were Erkan and I on the same page, we were ready to write all over it. What was originally an idea for a possible consultancy with a few people collaborating to make it a value driven proposition, was rapidly becoming an idea for a movement.

I am not sure exactly when I reached my own tipping point, but around about September 2012 I was waking up each morning with a mission. The vision was set, my contribution was clear. The need was out there, and I was going into partnership with 'that patronising sales guy from the NLP course'.

No one was more surprised than me! Erkan had woken in me a desire to create something that could scale-up to involve bigger and bigger projects. If we could show that collaboration from within a contextual culture could have a systemic impact on a small community, imagine what could be produced on a large scale. Sometimes the potential is overwhelming, but to not even consider working towards it would be devastating. I was determined to quit playing small. This was no longer a business, it was a mission, with no opt-out clause. It has become my way of life; To demonstrate what collaboration in action looks like, how to have a contextual conversation, constantly looking and finding the win/win and encouraging others to dip their toe into this new paradigm, to move away from scarcity to abundance, from fear to love.

This was the missing piece of my jigsaw. I was in. I now had a mission, and it felt good. BeCollaboration was born.

BEing in Collaboration

I used to describe Erkan as a kind of Peter Pan character, full of energy, brave in the face of adversity, not caring for the opinions of others and full of mischief. He loves the idea of being a rebel, standing against the establishment, being provocative and challenging. In the past few years he admits that he has matured. I think it is true to say that every Collaborator within the community has grown personally as a result of mixing with others who are not prepared to accept the status quo. Understanding the power of the community acknowledges the powerful impact it has on every one of us, including Erkan and myself.

I would now describe Erkan as having the same traits but also a greater ability to listen, and a willingness to share his genius to support the community. He no longer needs to prove himself like the 'intense and opinionated' man I first met.

We have both had some tragic personal challenges since we first met and I believe that because we had such a shared vision, it was easy to shorthand the compassion and support each other without the need for protracted dialogue and counselling sessions. I believe I am a stronger person for having him as a friend, and we both know that our driven mission ties us together for a lifetime.

What I love about him is that even if we disagree – which is rare - we work hard to ensure that our core values and vision inform our conversation and we collaborate to bring it to a solution that is for the benefit of all: a win/win. There is no space for one-upmanship, ego or scoring points. There is no value in 'I'm right you're wrong'. The solution is the prize.

As a father of two girls Tyla and Sena and husband to Arzu he is fully immersed in family life. With his children experiencing a school system he despises, it is a daily battle for him to accept having to live in the current broken world. He wants his children's future to be free and spreading the possibility and potential of BeCollaboration is his way of looking to the future and utilising amazing people and begin to build a better world.

However, don't believe I am extolling the virtues of a perfect human being. We are all damaged purely from the world we live in, and he too has his faults, as he readily admits. Cars are his biggest weakness despite knowing full well the carbon footprint he is leaving behind, he understands the health benefits of a vegan diet and yet will not be giving up meat in the near future, and his fitness is always near the top of his agenda, but never quite makes it into the action section. For all of that, we know that his intentions are good and it is up to us as a BeCollaboration community to support and help him as well as each other so that we can be a strong and powerful force for good.

Why the Lone Nut? I'm so glad you asked. Have you seen the YouTube clip[15] about a Lone Nut? The crazy dancing guy who delivers an opportunity to observe leadership and how to create a movement. I identify with the 'First Follower' and we are looking forward to the time when we hit a tipping point and BeCollaboration becomes the community that people are part of because they don't want to miss out. That was how we envisaged our community growing.

Have a look at the video but please know that I aspire to be like the first follower and dance like no one is watching, but the principle is the same.

---

[15] The Lone Nut video can be found here at https://www.youtube.com/watch?v=256eKjULdgQ

The First Follower

My journey to BeCollaboration was from a very different starting point.

I was born in the East End of London to a father who was a Docker and a mother who cared for me and my sister full time. I had no business role models to inspire me. We lived in a tiny 2 bedroom flat with an outside toilet, no bathroom and no hot water. For my parents it was tough. For my sister and I, we didn't know any different. I grew up believing we were wealthy, not because of what we didn't have but by being grateful for what we did have.

My state education was through one of the first comprehensive schools and I became one of the first casualties achieving just 3 'O levels'. I left school at 16 with a focus on getting a 'good' job. I spent the next 10 years working for a local authority in the Housing Department, and being promoted into jobs I was good at but didn't enjoy. I thought this was what adult life was supposed to be like. I didn't know that it was possible to do something you loved. If I had been asked what I loved, then it would have been sport, singing, drama and writing stories, none of which were seen as viable career options at that time. I truly believed that people 'like us' didn't have careers in those fields.

I encouraged my husband, Alan, to start up in business: it seemed obvious to me, yet I never considered it for myself at that time. Looking back I can see how I was entrenched in a society that supported a male-dominated workplace. I suffered the attentions of misogynistic bosses, sexual discrimination, and overtly sexual approaches. Just surviving the office seemed an ordeal without thinking about starting a business in a man's world. It was the 1980's.

So when I fell pregnant it seemed the perfect opportunity to escape. I focused on helping Alan with 'his' new business and together we began to grow it into a successful office supplies company. And while we were doing that I also;

- Had another baby
- Ran a Mother and Toddler group
- Started a Ballet school
- Went back to college to get some GCSEs
- Qualified for a BTEC in Early Learning
- Became a Teaching Assistant
- Completed an Honours degree part time – in 2 ½ years, phew!
- Served as a school governor

- Qualified and started working as a primary school teacher
- Found a house for my aging parents to move home to be near me, so I could look after them
- Project managed extending our home – twice
- Helped fundraise to save our local theatre to stop it being compulsorily purchased by the local authority. We saved it and kept a heart beating in a local community
- Plus being fully committed to and participating in church life

I became a Christian ten months after our first daughter was born and so we immersed ourselves in every aspect of the church community. We ran children's groups, fellowship groups, prayer groups, was part of the music group and occasionally led the service. Not to mention being full participants in the festivals, and was on practically every rota: they always need people to make tea, it makes the world go round!

All of this was keeping me busy and mainly gave me flexibility to be with my children when they came home from school - a common dilemma for parents. I believe that this time between school and home is very precious. If there has been any issue at school, home time is when they will want to talk to you about it. If you miss the magic 3-5pm slot it will resurface often as bad dreams in the middle of the night, – I know when I prefer to listen to their problems.

Eventually I began to burn out and was finding teaching children who had profound problems was taking its toll on my emotional health. I became aware that I was not at my best. I needed some time out to re-evaluate my choices. I wanted to be doing something worthwhile, but the red tape and officialdom of the education system was frustrating and felt like I was being strangled. Stepping away from it, I can now see that I was loving the time in the classroom, making a difference to others lives, but hating the time spent planning lessons and freaking-out over OFSTED. The original reason OFSTED was established had been lost. What was a useful tool to ensure a quality of education, was now actually creating fear in the school community because so much rested on the result, especially funding. The pressure that was inflicted on both staff and pupils was ridiculous, and I could see it was damaging to both.

I was a lone voice in a paradigm of fear. I saw brilliant teachers being restricted by the system and bad teachers being retained because they did just enough to work the system and make it almost impossible to remove them. I felt powerless and angry that this 'system', this outside force was ruining the childhood of many children and the staff were being robbed of the joy of teaching.

I chose to have a term off. Give myself time to re-evaluate how I could best use my talents and for the first time to look at what I should be doing with my life, rather than simply float from one opportunity to the next. With more space I realised that perhaps now was the time to join my husband full time in the family firm. After much soul searching I gave up teaching: the red tape and restrictions were not worth the joy of being in the classroom. I embraced the world of business – and I loved it!

As usual, back then I was suffering from 'imposter syndrome', where I felt I knew nothing – everyone else were self-confessed 'experts' who apparently could make my business a massive success, if I just followed their holy grail and paid them a mountain of money. I didn't even think to count my transferable skills acquired over years of teaching and in the world of local government. Not to mention those picked up while having supported my husband along every step of his journey. So, I signed up to some business coaching and any seminar I could lay my hands on.

My Mother's words came back to haunt me "You can have every qualification known to man, but if you don't have any common sense, you don't have anything!" So true. I spent literally thousands on learning about business and yet I felt that everything I was being taught was so obvious, so easy, so ridiculously simple. Surely everyone knew that, didn't they?

Apparently not.

It was not until our business coach suggested I train as a business coach that the penny dropped. "You are good at this, you can do it easily, you are in your flow, it is your genius, you can help people, YOU can make a difference!" At last I was a square peg in a square hole. I had found my role in this world, my skills could be used in every area I loved!

I could see that being a business coach enabled me to;

- Help people: I am a natural nurturer, and nothing makes me happier than when I can orchestrate people towards the moment when that 'penny drops'. Whether it be a business owner who can see how his actions were destroying his workforce ,or whether it is a child who connects with a story as they finish reading their first book: to me both are magical, and I will never tire of it. Of the many personality systems out there I can be described as a Supporter (on the Wealth Dynamics Spectrum), [16] who loves to lead people to new experiences and help them see their world from a new perspective, to discover new insights about themselves. This is what truly gives me happiness

---

[16] see - http://wdprofiletest.com/home/

- Access continual learning: if you do not keep up with the latest innovation, you are letting your clients down, but I naturally thirst for new things. I am compelled to learn, it's like oxygen for me

- Be creative: you have to be creative in every aspect of a business, and seeing clarity in the future helps business owners move forwards, plus if you cannot write creatively and with quality then you will find it harder in almost every aspect of your career

- Use my degree: by understanding how people learn and the psychology behind behaviours I can support people more effectively

I was as happy as the proverbial pig in the mire.

What was also the icing on the cake was that I found a skill that I didn't know I had – I was brilliant at networking, a natural in fact. I very quickly established my prowess among Business Network International (BNI) and was asked to be one of their consultants. It wasn't long before I was looking after a region and taking them from number 35 in the country to number 1. This was a great (award winning) achievement, especially in a male dominated environment.

But something was missing. I was giving and supporting, and helping, and getting to speak to audiences of 200+ around the world, but it was all focused around making money. Nothing wrong in that, we all have to survive, but it felt empty, hollow, and purely based on a transactional construct. There was also an element of me feeling exhausted supporting others, while I had no one supporting me. I had to pay for inspirational teaching, I wasn't surrounded by it on a daily basis. When you are constantly giving of yourself and not being fed by those around you, it quickly becomes draining. I was having fun and meeting lovely people, but it felt like I was biding my time waiting for the next thing to come along.

And then I met Erkan.

Do you believe everything happens for a reason?

I was so entrenched by my current paradigm that he opened my eyes to what I didn't know I didn't know. He suggested I complete the Curriculum for Living by Landmark Education[17], possibly more for his benefit, so that we had a shared language, and could work with a shared understanding and tools to use for moving forward. In reality he knew it would have a profound effect on how I viewed my life

---

[17] Landmark education - please investigate further, you will not be disappointed.

now, and more importantly how I saw my future. Having undertaken many personal development programs before, I can honestly say it was a pure release, a freedom from old world views of what others thought or expected of me, to a space of wonderful abandonment of doctrine and creativity for what is possible.

What also surprised and delighted me was that I was already ahead of the game. Many people go to the Landmark Forum and learn that they have to complete unfinished business in their relationships in order to move on and create a future of possibility. Already following this ethos through my Christian learning I was already living in the present. Any arguments or upset I had was already dealt with. However, I could now see that this wasn't just an exercise to do because 'the bible says we should'. It now became a tool to identify in myself and others, showing how damaging it can be to live in upset, to allow your past to impact your future, and how words are given immense power which you have control over.

What helped so much was to see that right and wrong do not exist. I walked away after the first 3 days feeling free. Free to see the world in a whole new light. In the Christian sense I had been 'born again' without any manmade religious doctrine in sight.

My new business partner had already given me value beyond measure. But what was I bringing to the table? At the time, I would have been purely practical and made a list of skills I had and therefore what I could 'do';

- Networking strategies
- Building communities
- Clear communication
- Creativity
- And the ultimate – an ability to Collaborate

What soon became apparent was that although useful, none of my skill sets were essential. What was more imperative, was the alignment of core values and belief in the vision and mission. Who I was 'Being' was far more fundamental to the success of our new endeavour. Erkan delivered to me his vision, mission and core values for BeCollaboration. My ego told me I should be working with him to create this joint vision and establish my core values within the ones he had chosen. However, when I read and we discussed these documents, I realised that the reason we had hit it off in the beginning was that we were so aligned. We merely tweaked the documents and agreed the values with one addition 'Human Being First'.

Already I had someone who didn't *need* me, but he was someone who *wanted* me to be part of his journey. I no longer had to support him. Instead, here was my future where I would be working with people who were willing to help and support me too. My future, if you like, was written right into the vision document.

Over the years, we have been in wonder at the strength of our relationship, indeed like no other relationship I have experienced in work or with friends. Working closely together you might assume that there would be fireworks occasionally, disagreements certainly, frustrations and falling out. Yet as a direct result of having a shared vision and a set of values we draw on to conclude any dilemma, I can honestly say we have never fallen out over any issue at BeCollaboration. That is not to say we haven't had disagreements, they are inevitable, but they are resolved in a productive session, where we know we are working towards a win/win situation. If one of us were to walk away feeling they had 'lost' a disagreement, then there is still work to be done.

I think it is fair to say that we have both grown as a result of being in BeCollaboration and have managed to bring out the best in each other. To repeat the words of Angela Makepeace who in December 2013 uttered the now famous BeCollaboration quote;

'BeCollaboration helps me to be the best ME I can be'.

It happens without you even realising it. And it started with just the two of us.

4.
Building the Community

In The Beginning

Back in 2013 at our very first meeting in my offices in Sawbridgeworth, it was a very different meeting to the ones we have today. Apart from the vision, there was little of the format that we have today that was recognisable, except of course some of the people in that first meeting are still with us today: Alan Brown (my husband), Arzu Ali (Erkan's wife) and Baiju Solanki were there. There were others who came out of curiosity and stayed to see what was in it for them, but Baiju grasped the concept with both hands. (He now has the dubious title of being with us, not at conception, but to use his words '*at foreplay*'!)

As our longest member Baiju has been pivotal in challenging us to be better in our thinking and our delivery.[18] And so slowly over the months we honed the conversation of BeCollaboration, open to the fact that we didn't have all of the answers and that we wanted Collaborators who saw gaps to come and help us complete them. One of the effects of that openness is that many people questioned;

- Our goals – we didn't set them
- Our business model – we didn't have one
- Who is on your board – in the beginning it was on a voluntary basis
- How do you expect to grow without investment – organically

We certainly didn't have it all sewn up. What we did have was a vision to create a positive impact for one or many. And we had a mission to transform current thinking through collaboration. We wanted to change what it means to be in business, based on a culture of '*Human Being First*'. It seemed so obvious to us and yet to those who heard this early conversation they often thought we were mad, revolutionary or on a mission (which of course we are). They wanted to know where the catch was, where would the money come from, how did we intend to become rich?

---

[18] He is also one of the first to share the profound effect BeCollaboration has had on his business and his life.

We live in a world where people always look to the value in the form of money. They see business opportunity and wanted to know what niche we were working towards, and yet our perspective was about bucking the trend to take in the whole of humanity. We weren't selling BeCollaboration, we were attracting 'like hearted' people no matter what they did for a living. Indeed some were between jobs, some were entrepreneurs, small business owners, employed, as well as those looking to transition from the corporate world to a new career in a business of their own.

Fundamental to our vision was that we followed our core value 'Human Being First' and this in itself caused confusion. People wanted to be able to put us in a box, with a label, so they could decide our value, condemn or vilify, tell us it was already being done, illustrate how it couldn't possibly work, or justify their reason for walking away. Without a more open understanding they were nervous and critical. Those people used to worry me. Should I be listening to them? Erkan helped me to understand that they were living in the current paradigm of fear. It was they who needed us to be in a box, not us. We knew what we were out to achieve, and we didn't need anyone's approval. If they liked what they heard, then welcome. If they didn't, then thank you for listening and hope to see you again one day.

What had started as a limited company, was now taking on a more powerful vision. This was not merely about a transactional relationship where two people work together and the client gets a better, quality return on their investment. It was an alignment of values, and a mission for the greater good. Yes, we wanted to bring talented people together to have fun working together, creating something dynamic, but now we were embracing the possibility that our community were coming together for a greater good, to have an impact to a wider community. Suddenly there were no barriers or limits to what was possible.

Back in 2013, when Erkan and I began talking to more and more people we realised that there must be others who were dissatisfied with the status quo, but who else was ready to take action? It turned out we were not alone and through many conversations, people started asking how to get involved. That was when we realised we needed to start regular meetings

We didn't even have a name.

We agreed to have our first official meeting and we called the group 'Javelin'. Neither of us can remember why. At that first meeting, which turned out to be in the evening, a few people gathered in my offices in Sawbridgeworth in East Hertfordshire. We sat around with a coffee and discussed how we could take the idea further.

The people in the room wanted to know what the website was like, but we didn't have one. They wanted to know what model we were using, but we didn't have one. They wanted to know what strategy we had to sustain ourselves and create income; guess what, we didn't have one. They wanted to know how they would make money from the idea; - we didn't know. They wanted logistics, plans, projections, and answers. We didn't have any. All we wanted were good people to come together to help us to make a start.

The one thing we did have was the idea that through collaboration we could achieve amazing things – for individuals, for groups, for communities. We realised the questions we were being asked came from the current paradigm that teaches us all to think in terms of "What's in it for me?" "How will this help me, and how can I make money for me?" "What will it cost me, how can I use this opportunity for me." It was clear that they were coming from a place of scarcity rather than abundance. They felt they had to protect themselves from possible loss, find the win for them, looking at what it might cost them in time and money. There is no doubt that they all asked perfectly valid questions, but those questions focused on the 'Have', rather than the 'Be'.

The 'Do' was to come later.

BE   DO   HAVE

This is where the 'Be' of BeCollaboration came from. People who are BEing their true destiny, fulfilling their genius leave a legacy simply by who they are Being. They do not worry about the details. They start with the WHY and if it fits in with their WHY, they align themselves with the philosophy, and the people who are working it out. The details take care of themselves.

Our first group liked the idea in principle, namely, get a group of people together to share their skills and help each other for a win/win. But we wanted to take that further. Share skills, talents, knowledge and genius to create something greater than the sum of its parts. We wanted a win/win/win for them, for us *and* for the planet. We did not want to create a simple consultancy where a few people come together to work for a client utilising their skills within one project. We see that as working in the current paradigm of WIIFM ('what's in it for me'). We wanted to work with people on shared projects where there was a purpose, a reason why, an outcome that would have wider repercussions.

We wanted to create a space for possibility. We didn't want people to be hung up on what they did for a living, we wanted to know what made their heart beat faster – what they were truly passionate about and to come and do that with us. We referred to accountants as being left brained, often detail focused and limiting themselves by describing what they did as who they were. What you DO for a living should not define you. Who you are BEing should define you – are you loving, caring, philanthropic, adventurous, kind, compassionate, supportive or nurturing? What do you want to BE known for?

That very first meeting set the scene for many others. Some came along to the sessions and found that the philosophy, energy and atmosphere resonated immediately with them. Others simply did not get it. Those that did 'get it' were not aligned, were often caught up in their own 'doing', mostly in survival and deep inside the current paradigm.

Those for whom the meetings did resonate, were already wealthy, but in a different sense to claims of money and status. Mostly they had enough of what they needed to be content with life, happy with who they were and ready to give back. That did not mean they were living debt free, or even cash rich, but rather they were wealthy as a state of mind. They understood that health and happiness could not be bought and that Love is priceless.

Baiju Solanki - an early collaboration

In 2013 Baiju came to BeCollaboration with an idea. The community was growing and with it the possibility to make things happen. He believed, as did many of our Collaborators, that the current education system was failing our young people because, despite gaining a business degree or similar qualification, in general they were not being equipped to become entrepreneurs. He himself came out of the world of academia and had struggled to become the entrepreneur that he knew he could be. Now fully in that world he realised so many with potential were not being given the opportunity to grow and create possibilities for themselves. He knew that being an entrepreneur came from a way of thinking, something that he hadn't seen taught anywhere. He wanted to develop an event where not only could young people be inspired, but where they could be helped on the first steps to their success.

He made a request to our Collaborators for support and within a few short months he had a date in the diary to produce the first 'Wanna Be An Entrepreneur Extravaganza'[19].

---

[19] You can see more http://www.wannabeanentrepreneur.co.uk/

For the event, which I also attended, I noted no fewer than 16 Collaborators had given up their Sunday to support his vision to help these young people. Collaborators were everywhere, from speakers on stage, to those filming the event, or taking registrations, looking after VIP's or manning stands at the mini exhibition. Not one of them were paid for their time, and yet they believed his mission was valuable and were ready to help. Over 100 young people came to that first event, and it has gone from strength to strength, becoming an annual feature of life in Southend.

Baiju epitomises how collaboration creates value. He shared his vision, asked for support, created possibility from a space that didn't exist, and helped many, many, young people to consider what their lives might look like if they took the opportunity of being an entrepreneur.

We cannot measure this value. There was no exchange of funds, merely an exchange of heartfelt thanks. This is the value of being a Collaborator. Having your dream come true because others want to help and believe in that dream too. Without BeCollaboration, Baiju acknowledges that *WannaBe* might not have got off the ground. Creating that level of possibility is very difficult if you do not have willing supportive people around you. Here are Baiju's words about what BeCollaboration means to him

> *"I had known Gill for quite a few years and met Erkan in 2013 at a business course we both joined. Over the next few months Erkan talked about the idea of a group of people working together, from and within a different context. Initially the idea didn't really sound any different to other groups around.*
>
> *Yet during that time, especially towards the end of the course we were both on, the concept of BeCollaboration started to come together. Gill was very much part of the conversation and I was lucky enough to be part of some of the early conversations around what BeColl is today.*
>
> *BeCollaboration talk a lot about how collaboration happens at the point of conception, well I feel I was part of BeCollaboration at foreplay! My early thoughts about BeColl was that I knew there was something in this. I was not sure exactly what, but whatever it was, I wanted to be part of it, however big or small.*
>
> *Since the meetings started I think I have only missed a handful. I go because it just feels right. There are a number of things BeCollaboration has given me and these are, in no particular order, friends, insights, relief, reflection, challenge, opportunity, love, excitement, sadness, growth, mentors, knowledge, inspiration, motivation, connections and lots of laughter.*

The dictionary definition of collaboration is 'the action of working with someone to produce something'. What BeCollaboration has created is love, friends, trust and an environment where it is about who you are, not what you do or have.

So there are many groups and networks that bring business people together, the difference here is that, the energy created is one that we all would want to be in ALL the time, not just when you meet up for a few hours each month."

Baiju Solanki – Founder of Enspirit Global

Not just a business!

It was at a meeting at my house in November 2015 that the realisation was finally spoken aloud. We invited a core group of Collaborators to a 3 day session to discuss how to grow BeCollaboration and during the discussion, one of our early community adopters, Scott Campbell, voiced what we had known for some time, yet had not allowed ourselves to verbalize. He simply said, "BeCollaboration isn't just a business it's a MOVEMENT! We *do* all *know* that, right?"

Erkan and I couldn't resist smiling to each other. He gets it! Others were smiling too and nods of acknowledgement from around the room, where for the first time the realisation dawned on some, this thing has the potential to be much bigger than we ever hoped or realised.

Our meetings gathered momentum and we had a monthly gathering in Hertford on the last Friday of the month. Initially we had a three-hour meeting incorporating the introduction and discussion. However, we soon realised that the conversations that were being generated deserved more time and we took the Introduction for guests into a stand-alone hour at the beginning of the meeting. We also realised that just because a meeting finished at 6pm, it didn't mean the discussions had to. We found venues close to a social space (aka pub), so we could continue the conversations in a more convivial atmosphere. I remember one evening, where debate was lively and it got to 10 o'clock and Erkan and I were not the last to leave: we quietly slipped out while Collaborators were putting the world to rights. That was possibly the first time that I realised that BeCollaboration wasn't just Erkan and Gill, it was a community that existed because we started the ball rolling, but we were not essential to moving it forward.

Realising that this socialising was a very important part of the discovery process, we quickly built it into the format. Now if you are invited to a BeCollaboration meeting you will be able to spend some time socialising afterwards, and getting to know the Collaborators over a drink or possibly a meal, where business is left behind and you get to know people, their views, opinions, dreams and aspirations on a deeper level.

Within a year people were travelling significant distances to be part of the meeting. From Brighton, Darlington and Cheltenham, Gatwick, Colchester and beyond, they were travelling awkward journeys to be part of the community. It was time we made life a little simpler for them. And in September 2015 we started our London Group.

Collaborators wanted to know if they were restricted to one group. They asked, whether they could only invite people to one group, if they could attend two meetings a month, whether the meetings would be the same, and would they have to pay more? Of course all these questions were based on what they had experienced from other organisations. We said, "Come to one or both, invite people to any, the meetings will be different, but still with the same ethos". It was wonderful to tell them there are no rules. It was an exciting time.

Growing a community and supporting members was my forte and I found myself, for the first time thinking of expansion and how that might affect the equilibrium of the organisation as a whole. At a strategy meeting with a group of Key Collaborators we had been accused of being "a jolly nice club" without any prospect of expansion, whilst the business model and structure were not evident. The possibility of growth was, we were told, "laughable". One respected and well-meaning member of the group said "It's all very well to have high ideals and a wish to 'change the world' but without specific goals, ability to monetise and expand, you will be history."

Yet we knew we did not want to conform to the norm, have rigid rules and regulations, deadlines, goal setting, and plans of rapid expansion with every Collaborator having a price tag on their head. That was NOT what we had in mind, and to be fair it was not what the Key Collaborators were suggesting. We were clear that we didn't want to play a game of persuading people to join, to set a target for 50 members a month and apply pressure on ourselves to get more Collaborators, simply because of the income they would generate.

What if the wrong Collaborators joined? What if they joined because they thought they could use the group for networking opportunities or as a hunting ground for referrals? What if they were simply in it for the money? Where would our vision be then?

So, we added the London group, not because of the additional income it would produce, but simply because it made life more convenient for our current Collaborators to actually get to a meeting.

Erkan and I devised a more fluid agenda where Collaborators would have the floor to create opportunity for themselves and others. We knew that if we offered thought provoking content, an opportunity for Collaborators to share their knowledge, and a space to test new thinking we would be creating a community that could propel thoughts into words, ideas into action and dreams into reality.

An interesting side effect of this approach, was that although run on the same philosophy, each meeting has created its own unique character. Hertford was still for many the 'home' group and London became the gateway to the future. If you believe in the Law of Attraction, it will come as no surprise that when we first started our meetings in Hertford it had crossed my mind that world domination was not far away. Being in BNI (Business Network International) and seeing how successfully it had grown, and indeed having been part of that growth process, I could envisage a time when BeCollaboration would be global. I allowed myself to dream of a time when I could travel around the world and be part of meetings where groups worked collaboratively to make amazing things happen for themselves and others. I contemplated that, with the help of the internet, we would be able to mobilise pockets of influence and activity, all based around our core values, to ensure we left a legacy in every corner of the planet. The 'what if' scenario meant I was setting off mind blowing possibilities in my head and in turn to the universe.

- What if – there was a Collaborator meeting in every town?

- What if - there were a Collaborator meeting in every school?

- What if – these meetings generated peace, health, wealth, love and laughter in each place?

- What if – we could work with some of the world's greatest minds to solve some of the biggest problems?

- What if – we could raise the consciousness of the country and spread our being to the rest of the world ?

- What if we could teach the world to collaborate?

- What would that look like?

We already have a feeling of two very different spaces: the BeCollaboration World and the world we are part of on a day to day basis. The universe was already aware of my dreams and I'm sure Erkan's too, not for global domination but for a consciousness to pervade that stems from a collaborative mindset. If we can teach the world to collaborate, then we believe we can create truly transformational progress for future generations.

Too big to even contemplate maybe? That's for the future that is yet to unfold. For now, if I only make a difference to those in the community then my job is done.

Developing our commitments to Collaborators

As the meetings developed we were conscious that there was no Collaborator commitment, from us or from them. It had been highlighted by the nominal board [20] that there was little in writing to show our commitment to our members – it was never our strong suit to get the paperwork done, but we were living it nonetheless.

In return for a monthly subscription, we committed to:

- Open invitation to attend any BeCollaboration meeting
- Two Orientation sessions, contextual and practical to fully establish context, review possibility, stretch horizons and evaluate opportunity
- Masterclass available at every meeting to progress understanding
- Discounts to Collaborator events
- Opportunity to take the stage in the 'Know and Be Known' sessions
- Space to test theories and generate debate in the 'Genius' slot
- The ability to reach a wide audience if invited to contribute to 'The Quest' (BeCollaboration online publication)
- Reduced fees for 'Be Inspired' programs
- Reduced fees for self-publishing opportunities through 'Be a Voice'
- Opportunity to collaborate with other aligned authentic members
- Space to challenge yourself in a safe environment
- Raise your profile within the community
- Have fun
- A Journal to record pivotal learnings and dream journeys
- Have future thinking discussions
- Be part of a self-organising organisation – no hierarchy
- Learn from others
- Teach others

---

[20] When challenged at a board meeting one day, I loved it when Erkan was asked, "What do you promise your Collaborators for their membership?" and he replied, "Nothing!" Collaborators can turn up to a meeting every month: in fact, they could have turned up to 5, and the only outcome we promised them is the one they generate for themselves. What we were creating was a space for possibility. We cannot however guarantee any outcome; that is for every individual to create for themselves. We will of course support them in any way we can, but it is them and not us who make it happen.

- Share, encourage and support fellow members
- Be open to new ideologies
- Be challenged
- Be accountable
- Access to specialist knowledge
- Leave a legacy
- Make a difference
- Follow your heart
- Be inspired and inspiring
- Discover your genius
- Create a new possibility for you and your life

As we grow we realise this is not an exhaustive list but an organic evolving committed potential.

And in return we asked:

- Collaborators attend at least 10 meetings a year
- Provide special offers to Collaborators for your events where possible
- Adhere to our core values
- Share your specialism
- Support your fellow Collaborators
- Be open to new learning
- Be willing to accept offers of coaching in a meeting
- Show initiative
- Be willing to support the growth of BeCollaboration
- Get involved – be proactive
- Work on you – use your Journal to be the best 'me' that you can be
- Be aware of your weakness and search out others to support you
- Be aware of your strength and search out others to support
- Meet up with Collaborators outside of the meetings
- Take opportunities when they arise
- Discover your Genius and follow that path.

Since then we have acknowledged that there have organically appeared three levels of Collaborator participation;

1   *Collaborator – turn up and enjoy - Be there*

2   *Key Collaborator - Be part of it, raise your profile*

3   *Guiding Light Collaborator - Be active to grow the movement*

As time continues we have also developed an online community who can reach us far and wide.

Be Inspired

As we continued spreading the BeCollaboration message Erkan realised that many people were operating outside of their genius. Indeed, many were still only considering genius as a word that could be attached to an Einstein or Picasso and definitely not to them. He long held a dream that could now be realised through the BeCollaboration community.

Having spent many years ensconced in the Landmark teachings, he knew that genius was inherent within all of us, that it was genius that sparked creativity and was the springboard to possibility. It was the 'what if?' question, the connection that made everything possible. We agreed that a community who were connected to their inner genius would be so much more powerful, that the context of what they wanted to do would be palpable.

He began work on his first ever **Be Inspired** program to help people to 'Discover Your Genius'. It would be open to Collaborators and non-Collaborators, and our first venture was a 2 day transformational program for just over 30 people.

The first programme in 2015 was a huge success.[21] Demand meant that we delivered four programmes in the first year. We began to realise that Collaborators who had attended the Be Inspired Program emerged a very different Collaborator after the programme. We found that a Collaborator became more authentic, more inspired, in tune to their purpose and ready to make an impact for others at a new level. They were more in touch with their genius. Many of those people from the very first Be Inspired program are still Collaborators today.

---

[21] Here is a video I love that was taken during the lunch break on the second day. You can see from Erkan's energy he was loving the whole event. I was freezing just off camera feeding him the questions http://www.becollaboration.com/be-inspired. If you want to discover your genius you can find out more information http://www.becollaboration.com/be-inspired

It became obvious that we needed to bring the programme into the Collaborator journey so that it became a pre-requisite for delivering a 'Know and Be Known' slot during a meeting. That way we knew the Collaborator was truly speaking from their genius. We continue to develop programs for the benefit of our members and wider community, 'The Art and Practice of Collaboration' is an eagerly awaited program, that has grown from our experiences of what it takes to be part of a successful collaboration. Our members too have created programs to support the community.

5.

The Collaborators

Stepping Up

During the same period as the launch of the Be Inspired programme, three Collaborators; Dave Cordle, Andrew Horder and Scott Campbell had made it clear that they were ready to raise their profile within the organisation and start groups of their own. Before joining BeCollaboration, all three were searching for a home where they felt heard. They came alongside Erkan and myself and quietly got involved in the BeCollaboration community, it wasn't long before they felt like they had always been with us.

All three are incredible people, who support us in a quiet and determined way, without ego, hidden agenda, or need to be in the centre of it all. They are simply the backbone of our community and I personally would not want to be on this journey without them. We don't always agree, that is the nature of collaboration, but we always listen to each other and work towards a win/win solution. I feel there is no problem that we couldn't solve together. I trust them implicitly.

As we want to attract people who look at their skills and want to stretch themselves, learn something new, help others and spread the mission, it felt like a gift to have Dave, Andrew and Scott step-up and become our first willing Accomplices[22].

Not only were these men offering to represent all that we had built, but all three were clearly stepping out of their comfort zones, raising their profile within the community, and adding their personal approach to the BeCollaboration mix. We did not ask them to take on the role; they simply saw BeCollaboration as part of their business and intrinsic in their lives. Their groups were to reflect their passions and be a representation of who they were Being. [23]

---

[22] Accomplice was a very controversial title as so many people had negative connotations around the word, but we were not happy with military descriptions that have filtered into business such as 'Group Leader' or 'Director' and we wanted to encourage words to be reinvented such as Collaborator and Accomplice (original definition is to accomplish)

[23] Scott a marketing specialist became part of the Be A Voice team and the Communications Team, helping to launch our digital publication **The Quest**. All three are well known within the community and have outstanding reputations for supporting, sharing, and living the BeCollaboration philosophy.

New Groups

As discussions progressed, we highlighted Surrey as a good area to have a meeting as many Collaborators already lived there and would have less journey to get to a meeting. Dave was keen to head that group. Sussex was also identified as Andrew knew several people who might be able to help him build a new community there. Essex was Scott's stomping ground plus where I was well known in the networking world and so it made sense to have a presence there too.

Again, there were critical voices that could be heard. We had: chosen the wrong locations; they should all be in London; we had chosen the wrong people, and of course the usual arguments that it was too much to launch all three at once, but this happy band carried on regardless. It just felt right.

The basis of the decision to expand the number of groups was simply to make the meetings more accessible to our Collaborators and give them more choice, more opportunity to meet like-minded people. We wanted them to have more spaces where they can discuss, share, learn and grow. We saw no reason to increase the price: surely the more they meet and learn the better members we will have.

It was not long before Dave had found a suitable location for a group to meet in Banstead. We set a launch date of 21st April 2016. Meanwhile Andrew had great contacts in Brighton and we partnered up with Benita Matofska of The People Who Share (also based there) and again we set another launch date for 4th May. Scott is from Essex, and we had listened to some people who suggested an Essex group would be too close to Hertford, and yet we still had Collaborators who were asking us for a meeting closer to where they were, so he chose Chelmsford and we launched there on 2nd June. In less than 12 months we had gone from one group in Hertford to 5 groups across the southeast with requests for meetings in Swindon and Darlington too.

Dave, Scott and Andrew have been an incredible tour de force in establishing our new groups, but they have also played a role in a number of collaborations, such as the Coaches Team, that set about creating new products and workshops. I couldn't wish for a better group of people to work with. They inspire me every day and have maintained the essence of BeCollaboration away from Erkan and myself. They have taught me that this really is possible to spread the vision, mission and culture of our community across the country and one day across the world. They look after the groups without being brash, or loud. They are calm, thoughtful and purposeful. They epitomise the BE of BeCollaboration as their Being is unique. Neither one tries to fit a mould of what you might expect of a 'group leader'; they are simply living examples of Being their Genius.

Here they are in their own words;

"In BeCollaboration, I finally feel that I have found the community I have been looking for since starting out on my own: a place where everybody is genuinely interested in me as an individual, not just a route to getting business. I can share my aspirations for the world without feeling embarrassed about how different they are to what we have right now, and without fearing that people will call me naive or idealistic. They listen, and share their own dreams, and suggest ways to work together to create something even better. As with every community, the more you put in, the more richness you get back, so I like to make sure I get to at least one meeting each month, and more is better, because that means I get to meet new and different thinkers, do-ers, and Be-ers. "

Andrew Horder – Joyful Genius

'I really didn't know what to expect when I decided to visit a BeCollaboration meeting. I was very intrigued after listening to the introduction and within the next 10 minutes of the introduction finishing I had a conversation with an existing collaborator that was on a completely deeper level than I'd ever had at any other 'business' meeting. As I sat there listening to my first 'Know and Be Known' presentation, ironically the author of this book Gill Tiney, I made the decision to join.

I've made some amazing connections during my time as a collaborator, heard so many awesome presentations, motivating genius talks and also it's given me some wonderful commercial opportunities, working with amazing clients as a result.

But the most powerful part of being part of this community and connecting with an incredible group of human beings is that BeCollaboration has given me the space to showcase my genius of making a positive difference and go from an introvert to an inspiring force within a like-minded community.'

Scott Campbell - GIE marketing

I joined BeCollaboration because it stirred something exciting inside me. I've done lots of networking and usually would look at a new group and think "what's the ROI?" BeCollaboration was different. I sat in the room and knew that whatever happened I needed and wanted to be around these people.

People who were doing things beyond what they could do alone by sharing and collaborating. People who trusted each other and created an environment where they could support (and challenge) openly. A place where you could stand up and declare your dreams and where people would listen, support, encourage and collaborate with you to make them happen.

I've grown so much as a person and it's benefited me, my clients, my kids, everyone around me. And yes, some of those dream projects that will benefit thousands (dare I say millions) are really progressing and happening, with passion, joy and love.

Dave Cordle – Career Development Specialist

Building Trust

Currently our society measures itself on a person's ability to pay back money. In BeCollaboration we ask what would happen if there were no money?

How do we measure a person's capacity or value then? In time, we believe that Trust Equity will be as valuable an asset as cash or money in the bank. A way of building up credit where you are seen to be trustworthy. If you can prove it on-line then you will have access to transferable skills with others. One day we hope we can replicate this idea with a measurement of TRUST visible in the BeCollaboration portal that allows our Collaborators to demonstrate their best, not simply through testimonials, but a full demonstration of their true worth and value.

An example of this was seen when Baiju asked for help on the *Wannabe An Entrepreneur* event. Many collaborators volunteered to support the day. No money exchanged hands and yet 16 BeCollaboration members gave a full day of their time – and some longer, to be part of his vision. The spirit of togetherness and collaboration was paramount to Baiju's event and has become evident in his experience of BeCollaboration. To say we enjoyed the 'ride' helping at the Wannabe events is undeniable, but on a deeper level we were all party to making a difference to the young people, we saw them come alive before our eyes and to see a new future of possibility.

That's what we are about. Making a difference, no matter how big or small, it is our duty to create a positive impact for another. No matter what their background or experience I find their genuine desire to help and support each other is incredibly humbling. They all have different experiences of life, different needs and wants, yet they come together for half a day once a month and their biggest ambition is how they might be able to help someone, learn from someone or gift some knowledge to another Collaborator. The feeling of love in a BeCollaboration meeting room is tangible. We may start as strangers, as our guests might be, but by the end of the meeting we leave as friends.

The Universe has indeed sent us some amazing people. Here are a small selection of their stories.

Sacha Bright

Sacha Bright discovered through the Be Inspired program that his genius was adventure. He had followed his adventurous instinct all of his life, including buying the domain name of businessagent.com ten years earlier, but had done nothing with it.

Having identified his genius he immediately turned to action and began to build a new business. He wanted to be the first aggregated platform for crowdfunding in the UK. A mere nine months later BusinessAgent.Com was launched in a fanfare of PR at the Empire Casino, Leicester Sq in London. Again a Collaborator had utilised people within the community to make a dream come true. Sacha had tapped into everything from coaching, advice, support and investment: all were forthcoming from the community. Less than two years later he has geared up for his third round of funding and looking to gain a further £7m to grow the business.

> 'BeCollaboration has seeded many of my ideas. It gets me looking at things in different ways. The space allows human beings from different walks of life to explore, innovate and express new ways of thinking. Most importantly it has taught me to collaborate and not to live out of fear and scarcity. By talking to my competitors and turning them into collaborators my business is growing. Also, Erkan has helped me to understand my Genius, what makes me tick and operating within this space allows me to grow. Loving yourself, collaborating and working to a vision gives me focus and belief. This sense of being did not exist in me before BeCollaboration and I've seen many of its members intellectually grow within the group. When they first arrive, you see confusion and then the lightbulb comes on and all of a sudden their energy changes, a wave of consciousness comes over them.
>
> Many of us live in a constant hypnotic state of news, films and propaganda designed to sell us stuff. BeCollaboration teaches you to be open minded and look beyond all of that. BeCollaboration provides a space for freedom

of expression with no judgement and If you listen carefully you might just hear that snippet of information from the quietest most unassuming speaker you have ever met, that will change your life'

Sacha Bright - BusinessAgent.Com

Alasdair Ross

Alasdair is a friend of mine from my BNI days and used to come from Darlington every month to be part of the BeCollaboration community. He saw the value, understood the context and wanted to be part of it from the very first conversation. His support and continued love have been an inspiration to us.

'When I was first introduced to BeCollaboration by Gill and Erkan, it was right at the start of an idea. They explained how working collaboratively could change the world by bringing business people together on bigger projects. It could open the door to competitors working together for the greater good, which sounds counter-intuitive, but actually by themselves single entrepreneurs are often unable to make a big enough impact by themselves.

Now look how the movement has grown in such a short time. Fun-loving like-minded positive people taking a serious look at helping each other to tackle some big ideas. Being a part of BeCollaboration is like coming home to a family reunion every time we meet, but the greatest single plus for me was attending a weekend on the Be Inspired Programme and finding my genius, a necessary step on my own path to understanding my why.'

Claudia Agha

Claudia had been a client of Erkan's and came along possibly out of curiosity. What none of us knew at the time was that she was embarking on a whole new world of learning, and BeCollaboration became her testing ground for her complete mission in life. To see her growth and development has been incredible, and she is now giving back to the community.

'It was refreshing and invigorating to experience BeColl for the first time in a room full of people with exceptional talents and desires yet with very little ego. It was not an exchange of business cards or job title, it was an exchange of authentic passions. That spoke volumes to me because I recognised during my first visit that BeColl was an environment where I could be fully accepted without judgement, where I could openly express my ideas and my passion.

Being amongst that kind of energy is totally awesome!

However, the biggest impact BeCollaboration has had on me was during the Genius slot which Gill Tiney was taking. She played a video and a very strong message came from that which etched into my heart "what effect would you have on the world if you did NOT do what you were meant to do."

That one line was a big "ah-ha moment" for me. Why? Because it gave me the impetus to step out of my way and create IAMPowerful. For that I am most grateful.'

6.

It Will Never Fly

How many times in your life have you come up with an absolutely BRILLIANT idea and someone somewhere has told you *"it will never work"* or *"why would you want to do that?"* or worse still *"what's the point?"*.

And your wonderful balloon of excitement and energy gets pricked and you deflate and surrender to their opinion.

How DARE they crush your dreams!!!!

And yet we all cave to other's opinions don't we? It is almost too much effort to go against them as they can't wait to be proven right. It takes a very determined person to welcome that objection and toss it to one side. Erkan appears to be impervious to the nay sayers, in fact he often looks to them as proof that he is on the right path. He believes we are writing a new paradigm for what it means to live your life and he sees many of the objections as coming from a space of ignorance in the current paradigm. He doesn't ignore them, he tests them to see where they are coming from. A place of scarcity? A place of support? Sometimes a place of ego or frustration. The opposite is also true. We don't want to surround ourselves with people who have a totally rosy view of what we can accomplish. We are realistic, not pie in the sky, but people who aren't ready to work with us on solving the seemingly unsolvable are not people we give much air time to.

We realised early on that there are people who want us to fail to prove themselves right and people who want us to succeed but who aren't willing to be part of that success. That is all good. Not everyone is right for this journey. What we are looking for are people who, like us, are ready to disrupt, ready for a change in the status quo, who are fed up being given the same old stories by the establishment that perpetuate the myth that the problems of this world are simply too big for us to do anything about.

Releasing yourself from your impotence, breaking the chains of complacency is surprisingly refreshing and as a result I have learned to follow my gut instincts much more. If it feels right, if it fits with our vision, if I am living to our core values, then onwards and upwards. I can quite easily state, that I have listened to your opinion and I do not concur. Erkan goes as far as to say he doesn't care what people's opinions are. If a criminal told you it was ok to rob a shop would you listen? No, your gut would be telling you it wasn't right. Why would you listen to opinions of people who do not want to stretch outside of *their* current thinking? We have to test where the opinion is coming from and learn to evaluate new understandings as opposed to taking on board ego driven judgement.

Knowing that we have a purpose that is bigger than most people's (i.e. not the usual 'let's see how much money we can make'), made me realise that this community has the power to change lives on a massive scale. Erkan has been known to tell the room that he and I are in this for life. I never object, or disagree. I cannot imagine doing anything else, it is a purpose that brings me joy when I wake, helps me feel satisfied as I fall asleep and makes me feel humble and proud when I am at a meeting or in the presence of other Collaborators.

Of course, I am in it for life!

Yet I understand when people tell us – among other things;

- This will never make you rich
- You only have a sweet little club
- You need legal documents to protect you
- Your structure is untenable
- Your model doesn't work
- You don't have a model
- Your only chance is massive expansion
- You should concentrate on one group
- You need to get advice from a sales consultant on how to close your prospects
- You need to show people how they can make money or they won't stay
- You are using the wrong people to open your groups
- You shouldn't open any groups stick to one
- You should be nationwide by now
- You need more rigour
- You need to be robust
- Erkan should lead
- It's the Erkan show – he should be in the background
- Where is your hierarchy
- This will never work

The first logo

*Gill And Erkan and a
meeting in full swing*

The Orientation

The first meeting

The first Be Inspired

The first Wannabe

First video - Interview with Naresh Haldipur

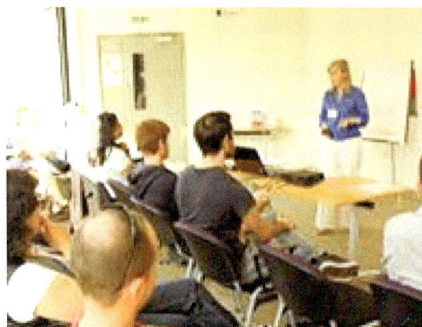

Gill at the first Meeting

Mrs Ali (Arzu) with Tyla and Erkan

Photo opportunity at the Hertford Meeting

Contents

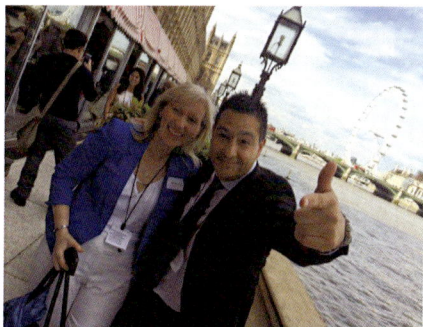

Look mum, look at me - House of Lords

Mischief

Staying for the adventure

Dave McDonald

Tyla's first visit

The Townhouse, the hunt for a venue

Bring your kids to BeColl day

Alan Brown & the Bubble Paradigm

Building

Claire Evens and the Yellow Book

Baiju's First Oyster

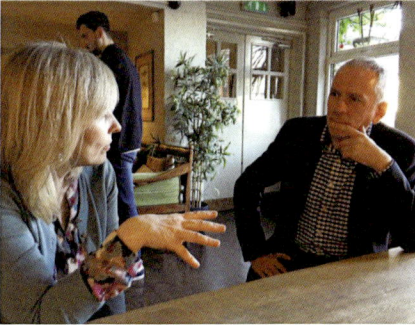

Andrew Horder aka the Joyful Genius

Challenging conversations

Mitch Herber delivering his fascinating Masterclass

Kids take over Surrey

Joyce Okakah - coming out of her comfort zone with her powerful message

The interactions

Nic Malcomson the peaceful psychologist

Go Create landmark session

Scott C. Campbell - Host of the Essex meeting

Sara Wilbourne

The Quest team

British Standard 11000

The Ashwell Girls

Hashtag Essex

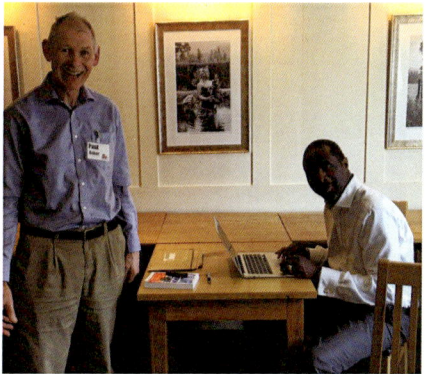

Paul Baker & Glen Williamson -
Building Systemic Win

Never say never - Aswhell ladies take the floor

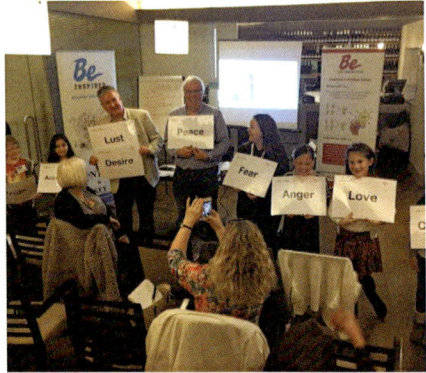

Having Fun and learning BeColl style

In the Studio

Its all about community

Simon Thomas

The friendships

It is frustrating for them that we are not building BeCollaboration in a way that they recognise or understand. In their world we are indeed 'doing it all wrong'. But for people like Ricardo Semlar[24] I am sure he would see us as perfectly normal. He has been changing the face of how to run a company for the past 30 years. He has been an inspiration to me. His delivery and common sense attitude makes me want to jump up and applaud. His Ted talk is even titled 'How to run a company with almost no rules'. Am I the only one who sees his self-organising organisation as one that seems obvious, valuable to all within it and created for the benefit of everyone who is connected to it? Giving his workforce choice, self-respect and the ability to self-manage, he doesn't anticipate people 'working the system' or trying to skive out of their responsibilities. He knows that when you treat people with respect and trust they respond positively. How I would love to have dinner with that man – what a font of knowledge he would be. [25]

Erkan and I are not in this to build a company and sell it for big bucks, we simply want to create a legacy to show the world how to collaborate, that will help people rise above the scarcity mentality to share their skills and talents for the benefit of all.

Mistakes along the way

Even as a most determined pair, we readily acknowledge that we have made mistakes along the way. Personally, I made the mistake of listening to the wrong people – Erkan less so, but we both bought in to the old school logic of having a board to direct and guide us. Our first incarnation was a group of well-meaning people who told us in no uncertain words what we were doing wrong. Without any investigation into our purpose they focused on how we would have to change in order to succeed. Have you ever experienced this frustrating condemnation of your business? Even our ideas of success were different. They were adding their viewpoint, not from a space of helping, but of proving themselves right, being seen to have an expertise that had to be qualified to confirm their superiority. The meetings went along the lines of the conversations the Wright brothers must have experienced – It Will Never Fly. They were so committed to their concept that we didn't even have to disband the board, we simply didn't call another meeting and no one made a single comment. That confirmed to me that we had chosen the

---

[24] https://www.ted.com/talks/ricardo_semler_radical_wisdom_for_a_company_a_school_a_life

[25] Having said that we have many influencers, both local and global. From cosmologists (Carl Sagan) to comics (Bill Hicks) - and some who haven't died before their time. You can find some more of our influencers on page 83 our research and insights spread from our own Collaborators to Martin Luther King and everyone in between. Being part of BeCollaboration is an education in itself.

wrong people to support us and for a while Erkan and I carried on simply working out differences between ourselves – looking back, we were becoming more and more aligned and so reasons to disagree were becoming less and less.

There was still a nagging doubt that most successful businesses had a board of advisors, and we knew that many of our Collaborators had a host of specialisms that we didn't possess and we wanted to call on them for help.

Not realising how much the concept of a board simply didn't fully fit with our vision we tried a second time with a new board. This started off so well with a group of amazing well-meaning people, putting in a huge effort to support us and bring us structure and rigour. We were so enamoured by the vast knowledge and back history these people brought to the table we were initially swayed to consider changing the organisation to fit their paradigm. We considered changing the vision and mission, looked at adding to our core values and even embarked on a massive undertaking to build a cohesive structure. We were determined to make ground and prove that we had something that was much more than just a cosy club.

And yet it didn't FEEL right.

Erkan and I soldiered on with the ever increasing work load whilst quietly questioning the core purpose of the endeavour. I personally was slowly drowning in paperwork and good intentions, whilst unbeknown to the board Erkan was voicing his concern to our chairman. Even the words 'chairman' and 'committee' and 'board' smacked of old school rhetoric. These words we knew were based on military authoritarian past conquests in a world we no longer wanted to be a part of. We were trying to introduce a new BeCollaboration language to do away with this old-fashioned hierarchy that didn't fit our ethos. Even this was criticised. Words like Collaborator (member) and Accomplice (group leader) obviously had connotations with the 2nd World War but we wanted to reclaim them back to their original meanings.[26] We wanted to move away from military language where control, rule and obedience were inherent in the words – such as deadline, strategy, leader, and expert. We wanted to find a new language that would underpin our ethos of collaboration.

We finally had a meeting that made us all realise that the way forward was untenable. The Board was disbanded and we were again just Us Two.

---

[26] Collaborator – our definition- **Humanity at its' BEST** A creative endeavour with 3 or more people that produces something of value that makes a difference that otherwise would not exist.
　　Accomplice – to accomplish.

I felt a strange mix of failure and success from this period. Failure because we didn't have a board anymore and there was part of me that felt this was necessary – old paradigm kicking in, yet 90% of me felt relief and joy at not having to sing to someone else's tune.

I worked hard to understand my feelings.

Firstly, I was excited to be working with people who I saw as hugely experienced and I was willing to learn as much as possible from them. However, as time wore on and everything Erkan and I had been working towards was being ripped down I was feeling dejected. I understood that in order to provide rigour for growth it was an essential exercise to examine every area and yet I felt that I was not being given respect for my specialism. As the weeks progressed I wondered whether I had a breakthrough to be gained. Was it my ego that was creating this tension? Or perhaps my feelings of trepidation could be because I was coming out of my comfort zone and I needed to push through. Or possibly it was because it didn't feel right that we were being taken too far away from our original vision. We were talking about BeCollaboration in a language of a corporate systemised business. Whilst that seemed appealing from a logical viewpoint, and to give us a place from which to expand, it felt too far from my emotional reality and my vision.

During all of that confusion for the first time I had considered walking away. If it was to become a corporate machine then in all honesty this was not what I wanted.

Fortunately, the chairman realised we were working from different perspectives and acknowledged that Erkan and I were not able to move forward, so he stepped down. Without a board my heart grew light. I realised my gut instinct had been telling me all along that it was not working. I had persisted for so long because I was in awe of the people who had been leading us into this new world of the corporate. It was an amazing learning opportunity for me to stay tuned into my gut instinct, follow my heart and make my voice heard. It made me stronger. It made me more determined to move forward on my terms, following my vision and not allowing others to belittle it.

What would we do now?

We had always acknowledged that we needed support to grow the movement and we called on our Collaborators to find a new way to do that without old school management.

Erkan and I discussed for hours and hours what went wrong with the board, why it didn't work, how we could make it better. He shared an analogy between collaborators and a guiding light. When you are in a dark space you can light a candle and it bestows a little light and you see a small way forward. What if you have several lights? You can see much further and can happily move forward. If we were able to utilise our Collaborators as Guiding Lights to show us the way forward how would that work? Not in the form of a board or committee but as a self-organising entity that came together for a purpose and disbanded until required. Not one special autonomous group, but driven by needs and surrounded by our core values and ethos they would come together dependent on skills, needs, purpose and requirements of the community. A true collaboration based on win/win/win. This fitted with what we had learnt from Clare Graves and in particular Don Beck who illustrated that the Teal level of Spiral Dynamics was where self-organising organisations had yet to come to full fruition. Therefore there was no rule book or guidelines for us to follow. Further realisation that our organisation was writing the rule book as we went along. We couldn't deliver in the same format as other organisations because we were out to create something outside of the current paradigm, therefore it needed thought and vision within the new paradigm that we were creating, through collaboration.

We were adamant that the work of the board would not be wasted. We had reviewed so much of our practice and could see many flaws that we were now able to rectify. The intense project based work would still continue but not en-masse as originally designed but in a more linear approach with a more viable timeline.

Whilst we hadn't yet got 'airborne' we still had faith that BeCollaboration would indeed fly.

7.
Remember - *It's Just a Ride!*

When we first started BeCollaboration we were both so committed to the cause, to sharing the conversations, exploring the possibility of a collaborative mind-set, understanding what it takes to work with a group and take the best of everyone - that we forgot about our day jobs. Erkan and I were still working as business coaches and the more time BeCollaboration took from us the less income we had. We were so focused on the mission we hadn't worked out a business model and as with most new businesses we were surviving on empty. At one point Erkan admitted he had just £97 in his bank account. That was the wake-up call. BeCollaboration wasn't earning us any money and we couldn't live from a good idea. We needed to review how we were going to be sustainable as individuals and still continue to grow the community.

And yet we had no intention of turning our members into targets for our future income. We didn't want to recruit on a numbers style income generating system. The thought of projecting goals onto our members, such as 100 invitations = 20 guests = 5 new members just didn't work for us. We didn't even ask people to join. We wanted people who were excited by what they heard and were ready for something new, not someone who had been sold to or convinced to join. If I had to spend time persuading someone to join then they were probably not ready to be part of the community.

Every person who has joined BeCollaboration have come to us and *asked* us how they can get involved. They have made a conscious choice to be part of the community. We were criticized massively for this view and to be honest it would have been lovely to take some income from the membership fees, but we had kept it purposefully low so as to NOT make it a barrier to getting involved. In the beginning, it didn't even cover our costs – all the usual start-up costs and ongoing expenses such as venues, website, printing etc etc, all normal business costs came from Erkan and myself. We didn't dare to actually add up what it was costing us – neither of us wanted to admit just how much we were losing on a monthly basis, without even measuring the cost of our time. When you believe in the vision we were sure the income would appear – eventually.

We had to consider how we could sustain the growth and yet still keep to our principles.

Understanding that we were the only ones putting ourselves under pressure really helped. If, as we truly believed, this was a mission that we were in for life, then what was the hurry? We aren't going to stop or retire. When we die we imagine there will be others to take over the reigns. At no point will we consider it 'Job Done' as there will always be people who will need to learn how to collaborate and communities that will benefit from the BeCollaboration experience. We would grow the community organically and eventually we would create some income. The rest would be used to generate projects that Collaborators wanted to support for the benefit of others. A benevolent fund would be our ultimate aim.

We moved our focus back to income generation and we looked to find more 1-2-1 clients. For me this felt so frustrating, almost a step back because it was a practical realisation that we had to provide for ourselves before we could provide for our community. Ironically it has been members in our community who have reminded me that in order to help others we have to look after ourselves first – a bit like the oxygen mask scenario in an aeroplane.

We both dived back into our client coaching sessions while still continuing the meetings, and as the community grew eventually we were able to take a very small income from BeCollaboration. We both continued to split our time between income producing activity with clients and building BeCollaboration.

It was then agreed that I would look after the membership and Erkan would focus on the commercial prospects of the community. We looked at our skill sets and chose what we loved doing most. We identified what we loved to do and chose that. Which is exactly what we tell our Collaborators – discover what you LOVE and come and do that with us. If it isn't FUN (a core value) then we didn't want to do it. Which is why I am writing the book and you will find Erkan in masses of YouTube videos. We stick to what we enjoy. That doesn't mean we can't delve into any area of the business but generally we work in our flow, the bits we enjoy the most, the sweet spot.

We do this because we are very aware that life is too short to do something you don't enjoy – even if it is for a good cause. This is illustrated perfectly by Bill Hicks[27] one of Erkan's favourite comedians. Whilst not my particular style of humour his now famous 'It's Just a Ride' speech sums up what we are out to achieve. Life is too short and transient, if we are complacent we live in our small bubbles, only care for those in our immediate family, do just what is required of us and expire at the end of fruitless unimportant lives. For those in the BeCollaboration community we are out to make an impact, share our reason for living, create solutions where none

---

[27] https://www.youtube.com/watch?v=oFHVkdxSzTM

previously existed and through collaboration create a better world. Even if you only make a difference to one person then that is worth it, but we intend to impact everyone who comes into contact with us, and like the wings of a butterfly create a larger impact along the way.

But, *it is just a ride.*

We must remember that if you are not gaining enjoyment from each and every day then you need to take action to change that. Putting off gratification for a future date is not rational thinking. You can be told this nugget of knowledge but unless you have it unceremoniously rammed down your throat you will continue to take your life for granted with a mañana attitude.

That was me until I had my wake-up call.

Life Events

In 2015 my godson was killed crossing the road. He was 22 years old with everything to live for. A girlfriend of 6 months, a fully funded new business about to be launched and a new home in London, a perfect beginning that never got to go anywhere. He had grown up with his family living around the corner from us, sharing weekly meals, the school run, holidays and fun. He was a fine young man and a good friend to our youngest daughter – only 8 months difference in age, the brother she never had. Tragically taken too soon. In the middle of BeCollaboration the message rang loud and clear – make the most of EVERY moment, life is fleeting, enjoy the ride.

Priorities shifted, for a brief time we all took heed and life slowly returned to 'normal' whatever that is.

Just nine months later his sister was knocked down crossing a road. Suffering major brain trauma she was in intensive care for a month, had surgery on her brain twice, and eventually came out of her coma. She had to learn to live again. From talking, eating and even swallowing to walking and functioning as a human. It took nine months before she could leave the hospital and every doctor and surgeon said it was a miracle. From a family of strong Christian faith where people were praying for her constantly on every continent around the world, she became our miracle.

Why do I share this personal story within this book? Purely to serve to illustrate how we all have tough times, we all go through pain and suffering. Erkan too had his heartaches as did fellow Collaborators. When we were hurting we turned to the community and the meetings to gain comfort and support. There were many people who shared my pain, had stories of their own, who I was able to help because of my own sadness. We were there for each other. We didn't pretend everything was 'fine' we were raw and hurting, but we were not alone.

Belonging to a community on a sunny day is fun and lively, thought provoking and challenging, but when life throws you those curve balls, being with people who understand your pain, share your sorrow and are with you through the dark days and bring you out at the other end is totally priceless. A lot of the power of a community is in how they help you back on your feet. I was blessed to be able to be open and honest, I didn't have to hide my pain, and I knew I was not alone.

When someone becomes a Collaborator we provide an Orientation to help them settle in to the community. Part of that process is to share a much loved poem with them, The Invitation by Oriah Mountain Dreamer. This held special resonance for Erkan as it was read out at his wedding to the wonderful Arzu, his wife. It has come to mean a lot to me too, and I can now say I have experienced the love of that poem with our Collaborators who have certainly been able to *stand in the fire and not shrink back*

You can see how creating a target hitting marketing campaign to recruit Collaborators was so abhorrent to us. We wanted people to hear our message and choose BeCollaboration, not be enticed in by promises. We wanted people who were aligned, committed and ready to take action. There are days in any business when you become overwhelmed with the enormity of it all, and during this time of shock and incredible sorrow I was certainly in that space many times. I can honestly say that BeCollaboration kept me moving forward. It was my reason to get out of bed each day, it made me revaluate my life in the context of BeCollaboration and made me see that this was the best thing I could be doing with my life here. I was truly blessed to be here, fully functioning and able to create something wonderful by building the community.

That was when I got serious!

8.

How Magic Happens

Earlier in this book I invited you to consider a problem.

The problem we all acknowledge, that the world is on a trajectory to self-destruction.

I believe that BeCollaboration is the possible answer. People who are ready to work collaboratively, want the fun of being around energised, self-motivated people, who are passionate about the same things they are. BeCollaboration is not a business community set up for networking. We are a fluid movement of connections that allow people to arrive and explore what they love, find others who will support them, and together make an impact that neither could have achieved alone. And that impact no matter how small is about benefitting others, whether in business or outside of it, for income or personal satisfaction.

In BeCollaboration everything from new forms of work, to conservation, mindfulness, education and personal development have been explored. And that is just in a three short years. Just imagine if we had collaborators across the world, who, through technology and in person, could work together on their cause – whatever that might be. Imagine if taking our passion and our actions into achieving free sustainable energy, food for the hungry, clean water for everyone, homes for the homeless, a new kind of politics, a new monetary system, or solve the education dilemma. Through collaboration everything and anything is possible.

Of course there are amazing people all over the world who are working towards these goals. However much of the thinking is derived from what we call the old paradigm of scarcity and fear. It is scarcity and fear that tends to block change by limiting visionary thinking because in that paradigm old assumptions run the show, and vision gets lost in the mire of political compromise.

Instead BeCollaboration asks how much more could be achieved together with a community of aligned, trusted and valued Collaborators all working together to create a space for possibility? By working collaboratively on the basis of a culture of core values we are more able to engage in creativity and produce solutions that will ultimately solve what we currently believe is unsolvable. In short, we believe that there is no limit to the change we might be able to effect.

As I mentioned earlier in the book the core and foundation of BeCollaboration is our contextual conversation; what has become known as 'The Grown Up'

Conversation. We wanted people to consider their 'why'. What is their purpose; why are they here? What is their reason for being? What we discovered was that many people were searching for their 'why'. They knew there was more to life, but just could not put their finger on what it was. This left them feeling, unsatisfied, unfulfilled, or just plain unhappy. Taken to extremes it resulted in depression.

When you confront this emotion you realise that you have to take action in order to work out what your purpose is. For many people joining BeCollaboration taking this first step was life-changing.

What I love about those who have become part of BeCollaboration (Collaborators) is that they do not put pressure on themselves to be incredible. Instead they allow themselves to absorb the possibility that they are, and learn from each other. They consider their passions, investigate what makes them angry in the world, and first and foremost learn how to BE. Part of this journey is about sharing how their current world influences them and shapes them, and slowly they discover how to bring themselves to what we call their 'default setting' – the part of them that became hidden because of pressure, of disappointment and the knocks of Life. From this place it is possible for them to grow, become empowered and take their genius into the world to make a difference.

That journey does not happen overnight, and it is not about a process that only happens to 'others'. Both Erkan and I have been transformed through being part of BeCollaboration. We have both started projects that neither of us would have even thought of had we not been in the space of possibility; projects that had been lying dormant within us and needed Collaborators to make them happen. Some of those projects have created amazing results for those connected to them. We have discovered that it is the community that makes it happen. Even the writing of this book has been a labour of love by the community.[28]

One of the aims of BeCollaboration is to create possibility. BeCollaboration affects people in many, many different ways, from simply enjoying the energy of feeling 'at home' to describing it as a 'dream come true'.

---

[28] I committed to completing this book within a very ambitious timespan of 10 weeks. Not ambitious for some but when coupled with my other commitments meant that it would only be written at weekends. Although physically doable but with a brain prone to procrastination, I called upon the support of the community to help me. Although it is me physically writing this, they agreed to support me via a WhatsApp group. Of course I would not DREAM of letting them down. Every day I had some communication to support me and urge me forward, and I would personally like to thank all of those people who took time out of their day to encourage me. You are very special to me and this book has happened because of you.

Collaborators' Journeys

Mitch Herber is a dear friend of mine, who takes time out from his very full busyness of life to attend the BeCollaboration meetings.

> *"I came along to my first meeting with a predisposition to the attitude 'not another networking group!' which quickly changed in an almost 'Eureka' moment.*
>
> *During the first meeting I attended, I felt an affinity with the 'be the best that you can be' aspiration of many of the members. I was also very impressed by the first speaker I saw, Hak Salih, and realised that this is a collection of like-minded individuals trying to contribute more by collaborative working and in turn, achieve more together.*
>
> *Areas covered varied from philosophy, coaching, technology, bettering our world, with the occasional 'woo woo' topic thrown in. A powerful blend of forward thinking minds that simply, I had to be a part of."*

Mitch Herber - Catalyst Image Solutions Ltd

Simon Thomas: Simon was a slow burn. He came to meetings and quite openly stated that he liked the meeting but he didn't 'get it' yet. He absorbed the atmosphere for six months before taking the plunge to do the Be Inspired program, and so his journey began.

> *"A couple of years back I was asked to meet someone new and, always intrigued, I met with the founders. I heard an interesting perspective on what is now wrapped up in a Movement, however coming from the Be (of Be Do Have) just didn't square with my logical brain. After another meeting, and following my instinct rather than logic, I became a Collaborator and now relish every meeting with any member as a learning and personal growth opportunity whilst returning benefit to the group with my digital communications knowledge. Having been around the block a few times I thought I was pretty content with my perspective on everything, but the diversity and richness of Be Collaboration members engender wider understanding of oneself, people and mankind, so taking personal growth to a new and exciting level.*
>
> *Where can you go where everyone knows your name, sees the qualities in you, many you can't always see yourself, where there are people with*

perspectives and attitudes to getting the best from life and what it should offer? No it's not a popular bar in Boston, it's BeCollaboration"

Simon Thomas – Director, Toucan Internet

Simon has now developed the blueprint for our platform so that one day anyone will be able to access the BeCollaboration online community. His genius is his ability to see a pathway forward and being an engineer he is able to consider every eventuality that our journey may take us. As a left brain practical person he was adamant that he would never be at the front of the room "waving my pompoms and talking about love, like you two do". Challenge accepted! I was determined that the rest of the community should know how wonderful Simon was and the only way to do that was for him to do a *Know and Be Known* slot at a meeting. He had been used to taking ten minutes at BNI meetings but the thought of taking an hour horrified him. Once he had done the Be Inspired program I persuaded him to come to the office to plan his K+BK. He performed with authentic sharing and surprised the room with his knowledge and learning. I surprised him at the end of the meeting with a pair of pompoms, he was brilliant!

Sara Wilbourne had visited a BNI meeting and although she wanted to connect with other SME's didn't feel that this was a good fit. During a conversation with Alan at a BNI breakfast session he introduced her to BeCollaboration. She instantly loved it and became a member – oh happy days. She immediately set to utilising her talents to help us become more structured in order to expand. She dipped her toe in the water and became part of the Be A Voice team and the Comms team, as well as pulling together the British Standard 11000 in Collaborative Business relationships plus putting together and coordinating the Working Streams to build the business. She supports Baiju as he launches a new operation and helped several members with their brand storytelling.

"I came to BeCollaboration by happy coincidence – but of course there is no such thing. What happens is meant to, and having left a big job with a global organization I was very at sea for a while. I found a safe harbour in Be Collaboration, a very different approach to networking and community building and was inspired by many conversations and discussions at the sessions. BeCollaboration helped me through a difficult time, and I shall always be grateful for the people I met there and the things I learned."

Creating Be A Voice

When I was younger I loved writing, anything and everything I used to dream of being a journalist, novelist, presenter and sharer of stories. I was told that 'people like us' didn't become writers and my dream was buried. Having written a book myself for my coaching business – *STEP UP*, I found it easy to coach people in writing theirs. In fact it gave me a deep satisfaction helping them to get their word, their message out into the world. What I had noticed was that many people have written a book, but not many had fulfilled the whole project and had it printed into reality. Exactly what I found when I wrote my book, it was relatively easy pouring out my story to help my clients but it wasn't so easy dealing with making it available and getting it out to the world.

My friend Mitch designed and printed my book and when I added to this mix Sara Wilbourne who proved herself to be an extraordinary editor, a plan began to emerge. The cherry on top was when Scott Campbell arrived and quickly revealed his skills as a marketing specialist. It would appear we had a team to enable other Collaborators and those with a message to share to help them get their voice heard.

I broached the subject with all three and was delighted when they all agreed to collaborate to bring this project to the community and the wider world. I have never known such alignment with a group of people who were basically strangers when we first got together. We worked for approximately an hour to evolve our very own Vision and Mission statement, which for me was a truly sublime experience. To say the pieces of the jigsaw fitted perfectly is an understatement.

We now have a publishing operation that can help those with a passion and a story to tell get it out into the world: a dream I had long forgotten but one that is now in the process of being realised. This book, in case you hadn't realised is part of the Be a Voice stable of books with a powerful message.

Be A Voice Vision

> *Be A Voice believe that every person on the planet has an experience or story to share with the world that will be of benefit to humanity. We know that writing a book is a legacy that leaves words and wisdom for future generations.*

> *Be A Voice brings to life great stories and ideas that have a profound effect on the reader that empowers and inspires them to lead a greater life.*

We do this with integrity and creativity by nurturing the author throughout the whole journey when they will experience transformation, empowerment and love.

That journey does not happen overnight, and it is not about a process that happens to "others". As you can see both Erkan and I have been transformed through being part of BeCollaboration. We have both started projects that neither of us would have even thought of had we not been in the space of possibility; projects that had been lying dormant within us and needed Collaborators to make them happen. Some of those projects have created amazing results for those connected to them. We have discovered that it is the community that makes it happen. Even the writing of this book has been a labour of love by the community.

My husband **Alan Brown** explains his journey beautifully;

"BeCollaboration is a group that is now part of my life. When I first joined BeCollaboration, I had a Bubble Paradigm theory about work / life balance. I had a passion to share this with others and a vague notion that others would be interested and maybe, one day I would write a book about it. This had nothing to do with my business The School People, simply just something I felt I could share with others.

Two years later, I am 18,000 words into the first draft of my book and have given many talks on the subject knowing that my theory will help others who are stressed out by this thing we call life. I would not have done this without the love and support of so many people within the group.

The friends I have made I know will be friends for life and to hear what they have been through and how they have got where they are brings tears, respect and love towards them. It also opened my eyes to the fact that beyond the outside skin, we are all human beings first.

Without doubt, I have grown as a person being a member learning from others and especially the life changing Be Inspired course run by Erkan Ali.

For me, BeCollaboration is a group of wonderful individuals who know exactly how to share love, enthusiasm and wonder."

There are so many wonderful stories I could tell you. In truth we are a microcosm of planet earth. Each Collaborator has their story of hardship to tell, each one with heartache and every one of us unhappy with the state of our planet. Yet they bring joy, laughter, fun and friendship with a zest for life and a purpose to leave this planet in a better space than they found it.

9.
Into the Future My Friends!

As BeCollaboration stands today we have a wonderful opportunity before us.

A small community currently based within 4 groups with a possibility for more, and with a committed team of Accomplices running them.

We have a Communications Team overseeing our digital brand and producing an online publication, The Quest, to raise the profile of Collaborators as well as the Comms Team and BeCollabration delivering high level quality articles on areas where we intend to make an impact.

We are launching an online forum planned to build and develop our online community.

We have the podcast – Journey of Possibility, where Collaborators are interviewed to share their mission and create awareness.

Plus there is our growing personal development program Be Inspired that supports and grows the community and The Art and Practice of Collaboration in progress to support others to work collaboratively. In my experience, very few people can naturally collaborate, because they are too busy worrying about what they might lose if they do. As soon as you collaborate with trust and the philosophy of always working to a win/win you cannot fail to make a success of the relationship, whether in business or not.

We have teams publishing books, looking at wellness, considering human consciousness, building products for businesses and with a growing community we have exponential potential for ideas and dreams we can't even contemplate yet.

Tipping our hat to the establishment we have been recognised by the ISOQAR and accredited for the British Standard 11000 for Collaborative Business Relationships, in itself a perfect example of true collaboration with Andrew Foy myself and Sara Wilbourne. Plus we have got the BeCollaboration logo trademarked.

We have a group of Collaborators who are willing to support us within the Guiding Lights philosophy and shine their skills and knowledge to help us make a better proposition for our members as well as supporting us in our journey to spread the BeCollaboration vision. We are aware we are moving into unknown territory for us by identifying our wish to be a self-organising organisation based on the Spiral Dynamics (Clare Graves – Don Beck) Teal level. Yes this resonates with our wish to step away from old thinking and embrace new possibilities. This can only be done when trust is implicit in the whole organisation.

If you believe in the law of attraction we believe we have already attracted some amazing people to help us on our journey, and I know these people will bring us to even greater accomplishments in 2018. Kay Westrap deserves a massive thank you as the dynamo who has transformed our website and created huge potential for us to move forward. Plus her true passion of Thought Field Therapy has been unleashed on our community and is already having ongoing amazing repercussions. She has come to the community and lived its ethos by supporting our growth and being known for what she loves.

In a few short years we have come so far….

And yet we still have only scratched the surface of where we want to be.

Next year we want to grow our membership, attract fabulous people to create even more successful projects, teams and become more automated to ease the day to day running of the organisation. Utilise video even more to create great content and develop more workshops and programs to support our members.

Like any business starting out, our journey has been full of ups and downs. I am sure you can identify with some of my joys and frustrations. I am not writing this book from a place of success – yet. This hasn't been written as a self-help book where you do as we did and you are guaranteed massive rewards. Rather it is here to serve as a reminder that anything worth doing is worth sticking at. If you are in business purely to make money, I can guarantee you that at some point you will get out of bed one morning and ask yourself if it is worth it. When it is cold and dark, you are tired or ill – or both, you will want to throw in the towel and ask yourself 'is this all there is?'

When that moment comes – and it will, you will remember reading this book. This book about two people who set up a company whose sole purpose was to help people to COLLABORATE. Who wanted people to work together to help each other so that everyone had enough of what there was to go around. They taught the community to work on principles of FUN and WONDER, where you could ask for help and no one condemned you for failing, only inspired you to take the learning and try again. A place where friendship and LOVE prevailed over every aspect and no one gained at the expense of another. Where the notion that as HUMAN BEING FIRST we were all connected and my win was your win, my INNATE GENIUS was available for all and where TRUST was endemic.

And yet even with these good intentions, aligned people and sheer determination we have still been thwarted by the current paradigm where we are seen as crazy. The model won't work, you will never sell it, the premise isn't right, it simply cannot be done!

In today's world of money, greed and power it won't work. It can't work.

*But we are carving out a new world, a paradigm shift, a new way of **BE**ing.*

I want you to know that when you understand your context for living, when you truly know who you are 'BE'ing, why you are here, what your destiny is, then no amount of criticism or hardship will deter you from your mission. It is your reason for living.

I continue with BeCollaboration because as an eternal optimist I have faith in the human species to evolve into a new world, where in our technological age we will move to collaborate for the good of all. Humanity can no longer be controlled by the few to the detriment of the many, we refuse to be ruled over when we can come together and create a global movement for collaboration. I am a global citizen, celebrating cultural difference in a world where no one person should have the right over the life of another. We have a duty to do whatever we can as individuals, groups and organisations to protect the vulnerable, support the weak and share the success of the strong.

If your business is going through a tough time, take a moment to consider why you are in business at all. If you are in a job that leaves you in dread every Sunday night and wishing your life away until the weekend then consider your why.

Why are you here? – do you know what your destiny is?

Why do you have skills? – and everybody does, even if they haven't been realised yet

Why is life a struggle? – doing something that doesn't fulfil you

In a perfect world, if you could help someone how would that look?

Can you turn that into your career?

Do you need additional skills?

Are you with people who will support you to find those skills?

A BeCollaboration the community will help you;

- Find your purpose
- Get you in flow
- Discover new skills
- Surround you with support

- Challenge you to be better
- Help you have fun
- Shows you that Mondays can be as good as Saturday night

Once you identify what makes you come alive you know that every day is one worth living.

And then you never need to *work* a day in your life again – EVER!

Because every day is a blessing and a joy.

As Angela Makepeace said when asked why she was a member of BeCollaboration:

"BeCollaboration helps me to be the best me that I can be"

For me that says it all.

10.
Final Thoughts

This has been our journey, if YOU are out to make a difference much of it will resonate with you.

One thing that sustains us is being crystal clear on the CONTEXT or WHY we are doing this. Knowing that BeCollaboration is not about us, not about money, not about fame, but about creating a catalyst for transformation spurs us on to greater adventures every day.

If your dream, ambition, mission or cause is BIG enough, it will take everything. Be prepared to go where others dare not venture, to be unreasonable with yourself and others in both word and actions.

We found stumbling points, in the resignation and cynicism of others, sometimes those others are your colleagues, friends, family or even strangers. Others cannot always see what you see, they will tell you with no uncertainty that it will not work, they will give you advice and walk on, leaving you walking alone. Going to sleep obsessed, waking up re-energised and passionate again, yet often feeling lonely dejected and fearful, and at other times elated, excited and infinitely resourceful Be prepared for the roller coaster.

You will learn much about yourself, where you crumble and at times feeling like you want to retreat into the safety and protection of your comfort zone. We say become comfortable with discomfort, make 'time' your friend, make failure your feedback loop, only like this will you take ground, only like this will others see your determination and dare to venture with you.

In our Collaboration both of us have given freely, taken when needed, and appreciated wholeheartedly the life force that is the gift of another human spirit. Our story is still relatively early in the grand scale of our aspirations, yet without our vision and determination we might have given up already.

For us the journey has been collaboration in action, every step of the way. We see it in every email, meeting, conversation and presentation, in short, we both love what we are expressing and love that we have chosen each other to fulfill on our vision.

Working in flow is where the magic happens, we are blessed to have found each other to create the BeCollaboration message and spend every day doing what we love in an ever-growing like hearted community.

With love Gill Tiney and Erkan Ali

Ready To Take Action?

If you would like to attend a BeCollaboration meeting
and meet our inspiring community, simply go to:

www.becollaboration.com

Find a location near you and book in.
Be our guest, first visit is free.

To connect online you can find us on the Facebook Group
Journey of Possibility
https://www.facebook.com/groups/1474370782583321

Our podcast Journey of Possibility
can be found on YouTube
https://www.youtube.com/watch?v=QDKWFPn-cnU&t=562s

Our digital publication The Quest
Can be found on Issuu
https://issuu.com/becollaboration.com/docs/the_quest_v2_v1
And also on our website
www.becollaboration.com

Or you can contact Gill and Erkan via email
team@becollaboration.com

We look forward to connecting up soon and learning
more about YOU and your vision for a better world.

OUR CORE VALUES

Human Being First – Everything else comes after.

Freedom – The power of choice.

Fun – The joy of living and laughing.

Innovation – Solving the unsolvable.

Brilliance – Shining like star stuff, the universal currency.

Genius – It's our innate state.

Lightness – It's just a ride, don't forget to smell the roses.

Adventure – For the adventure of being alive.

Wonder – Without it, what would childhood be?

Integrity – Being our word, reliably.

Collaboration – Humanity at it's best.

Love – Acceptance of ourselves and others, it's all you need.

"Inspiring Collective Action"

OUR VISION

We bring together, talent, technical ability and visionary thinking to empower individuals and organisations. We are passionate about impacting human performance, we do this with velocity, compassion, humour and love.

Acknowledgements

Alan Brown – my husband who supports me through thick and thin

Erkan Ali – without whom BeCollaboration would not exist

Be a Voice team – Sara Wilbourne, Mitch Herber, Scott Campbell their publishing skills that guided me through

Whatsapp Group – accountability from the BeCollaboration community

The BeCollaboration Community who inspire me every day

For **Danielle, Nicola, Tyla, Sena, Emily, Eliot** and **Zara** – our next generation who have already played a part in changing the old paradigms to create a new one of abundance, connection and love.

Influences

We Think - Charles Leadbeater

The Shift - Lynda Gratton

The Pale Blue Dot - Carl Sagan

Imaginal Cells - Bruce Lipton

The Power of Vulnerability - Brene Brown

My Stroke of Insight - Jill Bolte Taylor

Ted Talk - Ricardo Semlar

The Shift Age - David Houle

Landmark Education

Bill Hicks - It's All A Ride

KPI Program - Daniel Priestley

The Click - Ori and Rom Brafman

Pendulum - Michael R. Drew and Roy H. Williams

Benjamin Zander - The Art of Possibility

Life loves to be taken by the lapel and told: "I'm with you kid. Let's go."

Maya Angelou

About the Author

Gill Tiney is an author, speaker, coach, trainer, co-founder, mum, wife and very good friend.

A lifetime of learning is now being put to use through her business Steps To Success helping her clients to be more successful – whatever that means to them. She inspires and empowers those around her to be the best they can be, to realise their value and empower them to make a difference to those around them.

BeCollaboration is her mission to reach as many people as possible and teach them how to collaborate, to illustrate how in our damaged world we can all change the paradigm for a better future. She is driven by a desire to leave the world in a better place than she found it for the benefit of the next generation.

It can be done,

We just have to collaborate and BE a Human Being 1st and share the love.